Media
Research
Techniques

Media
Research
Techniques

Arthur Asa Berger

SAGE Publications
International Educational and Professional Publisher
Newbury Park   London   New Delhi

For information address:

SAGE Publications, Inc.
2455 Teller Road
Newbury Park, California 91320
E-mail: order@sagepub.com

SAGE Publications Ltd.
6 Bonhill Street
London EC2A 4PU
United Kingdom

SAGE Publications India Pvt. Ltd.
M-32 Market
Greater Kailash I
New Delhi 110 048 India

Printed in the United States of America

Library of Congress Cataloging-in-Publication Data

Berger, Arthur Asa, 1933-
   Media research techniques / by Arthur Asa Berger
      p.   cm
   Includes bibliographical references and index.
   ISBN 0-8039-4179-X. — ISBN 0-8039-4180-3 (pbk.)
   1. Mass media—Research—Methodology. I. Title.
P91.B44   1991
302.23'072—dc20   90-25948
                                    CIP

96 97 98 99 00 01 12 11 10 9 8 7

Sage Production Editor: Astrid Virding

Contents

Acknowledgments

I'd like to thank Mitch (The Great Rejector) Allen for his help with this project. After a number of tries (six, but who's counting) I was able to come up with a book he didn't reject. And he offered a considerable number of suggestions (only 23), all of which were excellent, by the way, to make this book more useful. I owe an enormous debt of gratitude to Chaim H. Eyal, my colleague in the Broadcast Communication Arts Department, who read over some of the chapters and helped me avoid a number of egregious errors (the worst kind). Betsy Blosser, another member of our department, provided a detailed course outline and other materials that gave me some valuable information about what would be useful projects for students taking courses in research. Tony Fellow of California State University, Fullerton, also was extremely helpful. He made a number of suggestions that improved the book. I am grateful to Ann West, my editor at Sage Publications, who has been very supportive on this and a number of other projects. I would also like to express my appreciation and affection for my colleagues in the Broadcast Communication Arts Department. They have always encouraged me and have provided a warm and supportive environment in which to work. Finally, let me express thanks to my students. At San Francisco State we are blessed with truly wonderful students—creative, imaginative, and delightful—many of whom make incredible sacrifices to get an education and are, in many ways, a source of inspiration.

—Arthur Asa Berger

PART I
Research Projects

My Illustrious Friend and Joy of my Liver!
The thing you ask of me is both difficult and useless. Although I have passed all my days in this place, I have neither counted the houses nor have I inquired into the number of inhabitants; and as to what one person loads on his mules and the other stows away in the bottom of his ship, that is no business of mine. But, above all, as to the previous history of this city, God only knows the amount of dirt and confusion that the infidels may have eaten before the coming of the sword of Islam. It were unprofitable for us to inquire into it. O my soul! Seek not the things which concern thee not. Thou camest unto us and we welcomed thee: go in peace.

reply of a Turkish official to an Englishman's questions, quoted in
Austen H. Layard, *Discoveries in the Ruins of Nineveh and Babylon*
(London, 1853)

1

Guided Research Projects

Many people are confused about research. They have fantastic ideas and crazy notions about what research is and who conducts it. An episode of the *Nova* television series on quarks, for instance, showed physicists and other scientists looking for an "elusive" submicroscopic particle and using huge devices that cost hundreds of millions of dollars. When many of us think of research, an image of such scientists, or of chemists in a laboratory or physicists with a gigantic accelerator, probably pops into our minds. Or we may visualize a psychologist working with someone hooked up to some kind of a complicated device. We see research in these terms because that is how scientists, who we know conduct "research," tend to be presented by the media. But what about English professors? Do they do research? Or philosophers? They read books and write articles, but is that research?

What Is Research?

Let me suggest that research covers a much wider sphere of activity than we might imagine. The term comes from the French word *rechercher*, which means to investigate something thoroughly, to search for information, to try to find out about something that is of interest. Research is also, to the extent it is possible, objective, carefully done, and conducted using methods that can be repeated. (These considerations will be discussed in greater detail in a short while.)

It is in these respects that research differs from what we do, without thinking much about it, in our daily lives. There is a famous passage in a play by Molière in which a rich aristocrat

3

asks his philosophy master to write something expressing his love for a beautiful young lady. When the philosopher asks whether the note should be in poetry or prose, the aristocrat says neither, that he wants something else. The philosophy master then explains that everything is either poetry or prose, and the aristocrat discovers, to his amazement, that he has been speaking prose all his life. All of us, let me suggest, are researchers—though we may not think of ourselves as such.

For example, suppose you wish to buy a new car and can afford one that costs $10,000. How do you find the best one for your needs? You might ask friends about their cars. You might go to the library and look at magazines about cars or *Consumer Reports*. You might look in the newspapers for articles about automotive safety, new models (and their good and bad points), and so on. All of this is research.

This book will guide you through a number of specially designed research projects, so you can get a sense of the excitement that comes from actually doing research and discovering things. But before you start doing research, let me say something about the nature of research and the problems one faces in conducting research.

Aspects of Research

Discussed below are some of the basic questions we ask when we do research. Frequently we cannot provide answers to these questions that everyone will accept, but these are the kind of questions that researchers think about.

The Who Question

Who was the first person to do something (run a mile in less than four minutes) or the last person to do something (climb Mount Everest)? Who is responsible for something happening and how can we demonstrate or prove this? For example, who is "responsible" for the disaster in the savings and loan industry? Can we point a finger at any one individual or group of individuals or institutions?

The Why Question

Why did something happen (the Civil War, the First World War, the Great Crash of 1929, the Iran-Contra hearings)? Why do some people with AIDS live for many years while others die very quickly? Why are there so many homeless people? Why can't American automobile companies build cars that are as good as the ones built by Japanese companies? Why do people buy mink coats? Why are some people creative and others not?

When we answer a "why" question, we must offer evidence that an objective person might consider reasonable. Often we discover that there are a number of different answers, and it is difficult to determine which one is correct or explains things best.

The How Question

How does some process work? How do we solve some problem? How did a certain situation develop? For example, we might wonder about how can we deal with the drug problem, or how can we prevent teenagers from dropping out of school, or how exclusive colleges determine whom to accept as students.

The What Question

We ask this question when we want to get information, quantitative data about various phenomena. This question is often a "what is the extent of" question, but it also can be a "what is the situation or what happened" question. For instance, television stations earn revenue by charging advertisers for running commercials during given programs, so advertising agencies, as might be expected, want to know what size audience can be expected to watch a particular program and what the audience might be like. For example, a 30-second commercial aired during the 1990 Super Bowl cost about $700,000. When you are paying that kind of money for a commercial, it is only logical to advertise products that the audience might be persuaded to use. That is why the Super Bowl broadcast included so many commercials for colas and none for Rolls Royces.

The When Question

Here we are interested in time and the way time affects some process or sequence of activities or behaviors. We might wonder when some process starts or ends or when is the best time to do something or prevent something from happening. When (at what age) do children tend to start smoking and taking drugs, and when is the best time to give them drug and sex education? When is the best time to teach children to read or to enroll children in school? When do people make up their minds about how they will vote?

The Which Question

Here we have to decide which factor or element in some group of factors or elements is significant or most important. We have to select from alternatives. (In the case of buying a car, we might be torn between styling and safety features.) Which gene is most important in determining some disease? Which medicine is most effective in preventing some disease? Which procedure is best to follow after a mild heart attack? Which factors best predict success in college education?

The Where Question

If "which" questions involve choice from alternatives, "where" questions involve location. Where does something happen? Where is some grouping that one might not expect to occur naturally? Where is the source of something or where is the result of something felt? Where in the brain are the sources of some neurological problem? Where is oil buried? Where should the new state university be located so it will be most useful to everyone?

A Complicating Factor

What makes research so difficult (and so fascinating) is that we often find that all of the questions discussed above are all mixed up together. It is frequently impossible to isolate just one element in the puzzle; you have to figure out how to estimate the weight to be given to "why" and "how" and "when" and "which" elements.

Social scientists must deal with people, who are very complicated, often don't know why they do things, and don't lend themselves to the kind of "hard" or "pure" research that is done in the physical and biological sciences. And physical and biological scientists find themselves dealing with phenomena of awesome complexity. Researchers in the arts and humanities have to deal with the still mysterious phenomenon of creativity and related factors.

In short, every researcher faces difficulties, whether in the physical or biological sciences, the social sciences, the arts and humanities, or the business world. Although we have discovered a great deal, there is an enormous amount we don't know—and, ironically, the more we discover, the more questions we raise for other researchers.

The Game Element in Research

You may have noticed that this book talks about research in terms such as *discover* and *excitement.* That is because research is best understood as being like a game. There is a task, there are rules, and there is need for imagination and creativity. Research involves curiosity, accuracy, honesty, and ingenuity. Research is a process, an activity that involves thinking up interesting projects to work on and discovering ways of finding answers to questions—ways that involve ingenuity and imagination, and honesty in presenting one's findings.

The term *finding* is important. Researchers are looking for answers and never can be sure where they'll find them or what they'll find. The "detective" or "spy" metaphor is useful here. A researcher is a detective or a spy who is out to discover or uncover something that is, in some way, unnoticed, hidden, secret, or problematic. Researchers, like detectives, find that their sources sometimes lie, sometimes offer conflicting stories, and sometimes behave in baffling ways. That is why research is so exciting and why researchers often spend an incredible amount of time at their work.

This book offers a number of guided research projects. They involve real (even if somewhat simplified) research techniques, such as content analysis, surveys, and depth interviews. Each project has been designed so it can be conducted in a short period of time by all students (regardless of major) and at no expense. All of the projects present the same kinds of problems that professional researchers face when they conduct their research.

Many students never have the opportunity to conduct research. The most they do is a "term paper"—a library research project in which they investigate some subject by finding quotations from relevant experts and authorities and, in essence, stringing the quotations together. These projects are based on the research of others and are one step removed from the actual research process as it is conducted in the humanities and social sciences. Doing a term paper is a useful exercise, and a standard mode of operation, but it does not give students an understanding of what real research is like or an appreciation of the fascination this research generates. There is a library search (or documentary) exercise in this book, but it is slightly different from the conventional library research paper.

Some Characteristics of Research

Research is generally understood to involve observation. The difference between the kind of observation and information gathering we do in everyday life and "formal" research is that in the latter we are more careful, more systematic, and more analytical, and we generally deal with more complicated matters. Let me discuss these characteristics of formal research in more detail.

(1) We observe things more systematically and try to be much more careful about our observations. Observation is a key factor in much research, and correct observation involves, among other things, knowing what to look for, what to focus attention on, and what to ignore. Researchers may find ways to quantify their observations and may keep careful records of their observations.

Researchers also use concepts—ideas that help humans organize and make sense of things. Concepts do several things. They help us see relationships between elements that had previously escaped us and, in addition, they provide us with insights. For example, we need the concept "violence" to find a way of dealing with such things as people shooting one another, hitting one another, and threatening one another. Researchers have explored the relationship between violence on television and people's behavior. Does televised violence "cause" violent behavior in people? It is a very complicated matter, with researchers arguing with one another over how to define violence and how to determine whether the effect of watching televised violence is "significant." The matter has not been settled yet, and research on this subject goes on.

(2) We are (or try to be) more objective when we conduct research and interpret our findings than we are in ordinary life. Researchers who study how much television people watch (breaking audiences down into age groups, sex, education, and other factors) are concerned with getting accurate information. These researchers may not like television, may feel that it is junk, but their personal feelings and attitudes should not interfere with their desire to obtain accurate information about who watches television and how much television they watch.

(3) We must be concerned with how typical or atypical whatever it is that we are studying is. Is something we are investigating unique and unusual, or is it part of normal, everyday life? If we use a sample, we must try to obtain one that is representative, otherwise the information we get in our surveys or questionnaires (about people's political opinions, about sexism and racism in the media, or whatever) will be distorted and misleading.

(4) We must interpret our findings correctly and try to derive some kind of conclusion or generalization that is logical and reasonable. Suppose, for example, you do library research on the "punk" phenomenon. You read articles and books by psychologists (the punk psyche), sociologists (punks and social class), psychiatrists (punks and the absent father), and political scientists (punks and alienation). You should try to come to some conclusions about what punks are like, why people

become punks, and what the existence of the punk subculture suggests about American culture and society. Since there is always room for error, you should state your conclusions in a tentative manner, qualifying them—but you should try to find some conclusion or generalization of interest from your research. And you must be scrupulously honest about reporting your conclusions, whether they confirm or prove false any hypothesis you might have entertained.

People Are the Craziest Monkeys

What makes media research so difficult (and so challenging) is that people are so complicated and hard to figure out. For example, suppose you construct a questionnaire and go around surveying people. Any of the following might take place:

- People will tell you what they think you want to hear.
- People will lie—they won't tell you what they actually think.
- People won't know what they think and will just give you some answers to get rid of you.
- People will tell you what they actually think, but they may not have any information and what they think might not be very useful.
- People will tell you their opinions and these opinions will be based on information.

There are other problems as well. As a rule, we are not careful observers of events. Five people who see an accident might give five considerably different accounts of it. The brilliant Akira Kurosawa movie *Rashomon* is about the different descriptions people give of an incident. A notorious bandit overcomes a man, ties him up, and then has sex (in front of him) with the man's wife. Afterward, the husband dies. Everyone involved in the matter tells a different story: We don't know whether the woman is raped or seduces the bandit, or whether the husband is killed fighting the bandit, dies accidentally, or commits suicide. In the film we hear conflicting accounts by the wife, the bandit, the husband (via a ghost summoned to testify), and a woodcutter who observed what went on. We might call this matter of obtaining different accounts of an event the "*Rashomon* phenomenon." It poses an interesting question—who do we believe when everyone tells a different story?

Research in the Broadcast Industry:
A Personal Perspective

The week I started writing this book I was interviewed by a reporter from a local television station. The reason I mention this is to emphasize an important point: Research is not something done only by scholars; it also plays an important part in the media.

A reporter was working on a series of three 2-minute segments (to be shown on the late evening news) dealing with nostalgia in American culture. A producer for one of the news shows had noticed that a number of commercials had a "fifties" theme to them and that there seemed to be a good deal of "back to the fifties" material reflected in our popular culture. Her question was "Why is this going on, and why now?" (We will assume that she was correct about her nostalgia hypothesis.)

She called a number of universities looking for people who might have some "expertise" on the matter. She called the public affairs office at San Francisco State University and they referred her to me, since I have done a considerable amount of work on media and popular culture. She called Stanford University and they suggested she speak to someone from a local futures research organization, so she ended up interviewing a futurist. She called advertising agencies and all kinds of other people. She also found some articles and books that were relevant.

What she did is, from my point of view, research, and the success of reporters is as much connected to their ability to find information and good sources for interviews as it is to their ability to write and to speak well. Her particular kind of research involved finding experts, people who could speak (allegedly, at least) with authority, and what she did was no different from what students do when they do library research projects, except that she did not rely on books and articles by experts or authorities but went out and actually interviewed these people.

So research is not some abstract process that is irrelevant to work and to life. It plays an important part in both, whether one does research on what automobile to buy, on the best way to get people to purchase some product or service, or on how to get a particular job.

The Goal of This Book

This book deals with what might be called applied or "practical" research. It will lead you, step by step, through a number of research projects that will help you learn how to conduct research. The goal is not to turn you into a professional researcher, but to help you understand something about research so that you can function more effectively when you are working—regardless of the position you hold. We live in an information society; more than half of the U.S. gross national product comes from processing information. Given this situation, your ability to find information and interpret and evaluate it (whether you are a reporter, a producer, or an executive) is of great importance.

This book can be used in conjunction with texts on research methodology, but it also can stand alone and can be used in courses dealing with topics such as media, the popular arts, or American culture or society. It offers specially designed projects that can be done reasonably quickly and at little or no expense. The projects can be adapted or modified, depending on the needs and interests of instructors and their students. For example, in the social role analysis chapter (Chapter 5), instead of investigating soap operas some other genre can be substituted. In the same manner, the concepts discussed in the rhetorical analysis chapter (Chapter 7) can be applied to other media and other genres.

The detective metaphor is (once again) useful here. Research, in many respects, is similar to what detectives do. Detectives have a crime to solve. They search for clues, consider a number of suspects, and use any clues they find to discover the guilty party (in mystery stories, usually a murderer). Researchers find some problem that interests them, search for information, consider how useful or correct the information is, and use the information to come to some kind of conclusion or generalization. Researchers sometimes develop hypotheses (informed guesses) to test, but this is not always the case. Sometimes they investigate topics or problems that interest them, ones that they believe have important and interesting implications. The parallel lists below show the similarities between detectives and researchers.

detectives	*researchers*
crime	problem, topic
clues	information
suspicious characters	questionable data
discovery of criminal	conclusion, generalization

Why should students, to continue with the detective metaphor, only read about other detectives when they can be detectives themselves?

The work in the comparative study of lives brought another type of evidence in favor of using a personal journal as the basic instrument of personal growth. It was impressive to observe the number of persons in other cultures and other periods of history who have spontaneously kept a journal of some sort to meet various needs in their lives. These journals are primarily a chronological record of events. They are diaries elaborated to a greater or less degree depending on the temperament of the person and his life situation. Sometimes they are focused on a particular area of experience or a particular task, as is often the case for artists and novelists. In those cases a journal serves as the spontaneous psychological tool that makes it possible for the inner creative side of a work in progress to be carried through.

Ira Progoff, *At a Journal Workshop: The Basic Text and Guide for Using the Intensive Journal* (1975, p. 23)

2

Research Logs

Keeping a research log is a subject dear to my heart, since I have been keeping something like a log—a journal—since 1954, and have written more than 50 journals since that time. Most of my books, including this one, have come out of my journals. The term *keeping* is very important, for it suggests some kind of obligation, a sense of duty. You have to be faithful to your log and spend time writing in it regularly or it will be of little value to you.

A distinction should be made here between a research log and a diary. A diary, as it is generally understood, is a record of personal thoughts, of private experiences, that focuses upon activities one is involved with, hopes, aspirations, matters of the heart, and that kind of thing. A log, on the other hand, is much different. It may occasionally deal with personal matters, but the main focus should be on thoughts and reflections.

We will keep a log to record our thoughts and speculations about the various research projects that we undertake. In this log we will "talk to ourselves" about problems we face in doing the research projects, ideas relative to the research projects, what our findings mean, and things like that.

Keeping journals and logs is a very effective way of forcing oneself to think about things and to maintain an "internal dialogue." The "writing across the curriculum movement" stresses the role that writing, and in particular journals and logs, can play in all courses—whether or not these are specifically designed as writing courses. For example, students in physics courses can record their thinking as they work on problems. When instructors examine students' logs, they can see how the students dealt with the problems, see the way their minds worked. If a student made an error, it will be reflected in his or her log.

15

In the first chapter of *Improving Student Writing: A Guidebook for Faculty in All Disciplines,* Andrew Moss and Carol Holder (1988) discuss the value of writing:

> Whatever kinds of writing tasks you are at present assigning your students—research papers, essay exams, lab reports, book critiques, journals—your assignments are giving them a unique and valuable opportunity to learn. Through writing, students can learn to review and reflect upon the ideas they express, can learn to analyze concepts and see their relationships to one another. Unlike conversation, writing creates a visible record that one can ponder, add to, or revise. By challenging students to be analytical and reflective, well conceived writing assignments deepen their understanding of any field, enabling them to create meaning out of raw data and express that meaning intelligently to others. (p. 1)

What these authors say about writing in general is particularly relevant to the matter of keeping research logs.

Difficulties in Log Writing

You must be disciplined about keeping a log—that is, you must write in it regularly. One thing you will discover, if you get into keeping a log, is that frequently the process of writing seems to take over and all kinds of ideas, notions, and solutions to difficulties that were not in your consciousness when you started pop into your mind. As you become involved with the writing, many of your inhibitions ("that's a silly idea" or "that's too far out") slip away and you have access, somehow, to parts of your unconscious.

You have to be honest with yourself as you write in your log. You must be willing to record things like difficulties, errors you may have made in some part of some research project, and problems you face. It is often difficult for people to do this. Also, you may find that your progress is uneven—sometimes things go well, other times everything goes wrong. Your log should reflect all this.

Advantages of Logs

Logs are very "immediate," reflecting things as they evolve. As a result, you have a record of how you progressed as you worked on each of the various research projects assigned to you. You can speculate on how things are going, record what you have found, consider various aspects of your research. This material will be very useful to you when you have to "write up" your findings.

Logs are inexpensive and do not take a great deal of time. All you need is a bound laboratory notebook with numbered pages, a pen, and 10 or 15 minutes every day. What is important is that you write in your log regularly, not that you write in it for long periods of time. When you are done with the log, you will have an excellent record of your experiences in the course and you may have ideas that can be developed into other research projects, future papers, and that kind of thing.

Guidelines for Keeping a Log

The following guidelines are based on my years of keeping journals and reflect my personal notions of how one should keep a journal or a log. There is no one way to keep a log, and your instructors may have their own ideas about journals and logs.

(1) Keep your log in a bound notebook with numbered pages. You must not be able to tear pages out or add pages. Having the pages numbered means you can keep an index in the back of the book and be able to find what you have written in the log with relative ease.

(2) Write in ink. It is much easier to read. You can cross words out and be messy if you want. Neatness is not a critical factor. And write directly into the log; don't write things out on a piece of paper and copy what you have written into your log. It is better to spend 20 minutes writing (and thinking) in a messy manner than 10 minutes writing something and another 10 minutes

copying what you have written into your log. This is boring and
wastes your time.

(3) Note the date each time you write. This enables you to see, at a
later date, how you were progressing and when you were involved with various parts of each research project.

(4) Make use of diagrams and charts. These show relationships and
can be very useful in helping you gain insights and come to
conclusions.

(5) Use modified outlines when you are brainstorming. You can
divide a page into three or four vertical columns, for example,
and do a great deal of brainstorming up and down the columns.
You can also number the ideas you generate—then, later, you can
take some of these ideas and put them into a more logical or
useful order. You might want to keep lists of things to do when
doing your content analysis or some other project. Or you may
want to think of ideas to deal with for a write-up of some project.

(6) Write headlines in your logs in all caps when you have a specific
topic that you are thinking about. This enables you to keep a
better index, and having a headline to focus your thinking can
also help you to think more clearly.

(7) Do small spot drawings, of an inch or inch and a half square,
from time to time. These drawings give your log visual appeal.
When they are related to your topic, they may also help stimulate
your imagination and thinking.

A Case Study

You may find it interesting to see how notes in a writer's
journal or log evolved into a book. A number of years ago, when
I was deeply involved in semiotics (the science of signs) I
started a journal and, appropriately, called it *The Sign*. (I always
give my journals names, for some reason.) In this journal I
devoted page after page to speculating about different aspects
of signs. I spent weeks thinking of all the things I might write
about signs. In the journal I wrote many pages of lists, charts,
speculations, topics—anything that came into my head that
was related to semiotics.

Once I had done this preliminary "thinking," I decided to
write a short book, of 70 or 80 pages, based on these ideas.
I was offering a seminar in semiotics and the media, and I

thought my students would find the book useful. Using the material—the notes, the charts, the diagrams, the speculations—in my journal as an outline, I wrote a book, *The Sign*, which was duplicated by the campus bookstore, and used it in my seminar.

I later sent a copy of *The Sign* to an editor who was looking for manuscripts on the media, and he suggested I might want to expand it into a real book, which I was more than happy to do. So my journal led to *The Sign* and *The Sign* led to a book, *Signs in Contemporary Culture: An Introduction to Semiotics*, which was published by Annenberg-Longman (Berger, 1984).

Figures 2.1, 2.2, and 2.3 present reproductions of, respectively, a page from my journal, a page from the duplicated book *The Sign*, and a page from *Signs in Contemporary Culture*. And *Signs in Contemporary Culture*, let me add, is no different from any of my other books—they all sprung from my journals. The moral of this disquisition, then, is that you should keep a good log for the course for which this book was assigned—and if you think the process is useful, start keeping your own journal.

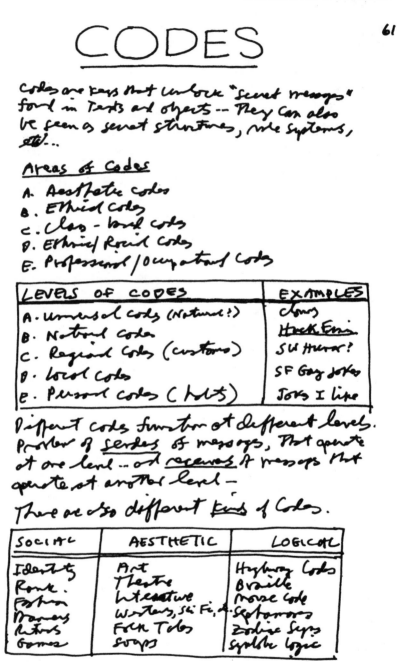

Figure 2.1. Page from Journal Used to Write *The Sign* and *Signs in Contemporary Culture*

10. Levels of Codes

One of the problems we face in dealing with codes stems from the
fact that they can operate at different levels--sometimes at the same
time, also. Think of humor, for example. Some humor is universal--
things like the antics of clowns or mimes. Other humor seems to be
national or, at least, deeply affected by matters connected with
nations. Here I'm thinking of English understatement, American exuber-
ance, etc. Then, within nations, there are other subcategories such as
regional humor (Yankee, Southern), local humor (Bostonian) and
individual humor (a given person's sense of humor).

In the chart that follows I have categorized the levels of humor,
offered explanations of what causes them, and given examples.

Level	Explanation	Example
Universal	Natural	Mimes, Clowns
National	History	American Characters
Regional	Geography	Country Bumpkin
Local	Groups	Jokes about Gays in S.F.
Individual	Personality	Jokes I like

Code Levels

The fact that these code levels exist means that there is often a
great deal of confusion caused by, for instance, a sender of a message
operating at one level and a receiver of a message operating at another
level. In addition, matters such as educational level, ethnicity

Figure 2.2. Page from Typed Manuscript, *The Sign*

Then, within nations, there are other subcategories such as regional humor (Yankee, Southern), local humor (Bostonian) and individual humor (a given person's sense of humor). In the chart that follows I've categorized the levels of humor, offered explanations of what causes them, and given examples.

Code Levels

Level	Explanation	Example
Universal	Nature	Mimes
National	History	American Characters, e.g. Huck Finn
Regional	Geography	Country Bumpkin vs. City Slicker
Local	Groups	Jokes about gays in San Francisco
Individual	Personality	Jokes I like

The fact that different code levels exist means that there can be a great deal of confusion. For instance, the sender of a message can be operating at one level but the receiver of the message operating at another. In addition, factors such as educational level, ethnicity, social class, and race play a role and further complicate communication.

There is also the matter of kinds of codes. It has been suggested by the French semiologist Pierre Guiraud, in his book, *Semiology*, that there are three important kinds of codes: social codes, aesthetic codes, and logical codes.

The attributes and characteristics of these codes are found in the following chart.

Kinds of Codes

Social Codes	Aesthetic Codes	Logical Codes
Relations Among Men and Women in Society	Interpreting and Evaluating Arts and Literature	Understanding Nature and the World
Identity	Art	Highway Code
Rank	Literature	Symbolic Logic
Manners	Theatre	Braille
Fashion	Comic Strips	Morse Code
Rituals	Westerns	Sign Language
Greetings	Folk Tales	Sephamores
Games	Soap Operas	Zodiac Signs

Figure 2.3. Page from *Signs in Contemporary Culture*

SOURCE: Berger (1984). Copyright 1984 by Sheffield Publishing Co. Reprinted by permission.

Content analysis is a research technique for the systematic classification and description of communication content according to certain usually predetermined categories. It may involve quantitative or qualitative analysis, or both. Technical objectivity requires that the categories of classification and analysis be clearly and operationally defined so that other researchers can follow them reliably. For example, analysis of the social class memberships of television characters requires clear specification of the criteria by which class is identified and classified, so that independent coders are likely to agree on how to classify a character. . . . It is important to remember, however, that content analysis itself provides no direct data about the nature of the communicator, audience, or effects. Therefore, great caution must be exercised whenever this technique is used for any purpose other than the classification, description, and analysis of the manifest content of the communication.

Charles R. Wright, *Mass Communication: A Sociological Perspective*
(1986, pp. 125-126)

3

Content Analysis: Newspaper Comics Pages

Content analysis, as the term will be used here, is a research technique that is based on measuring the amount of something (violence, negative portrayals of women, or whatever) in a representative sampling of some mass-mediated popular art form, such as a newspaper comic strip. (One can also conduct content analyses of phenomena such as personal letters, telephone conversations, and classroom lectures, which are not mass mediated.)

As George V. Zito writes in *Methodology and Meanings: Varieties of Sociological Inquiry* (1975):

> Content analysis may be defined as a methodology by which the researcher seeks to determine the manifest content of written, spoken, or published communications by *systematic, objective*, and *quantitative* analysis. . . . Since any written communication (and this includes novels, plays, and television scripts as well as personal letters, suicide notes, magazines, and newspaper accounts) is produced by a communicator, the *intention of the communicator* may be the object of our research. Or we may be interested in the audience, or *receiver* of the communication, and may attempt to determine something about it. (p. 27)

Content analysis is a means of trying to learn something about people by examining what they write, produce on television, or make movies about. Content analysts assume that behavioral patterns, values, and attitudes found in this material reflect and affect the behaviors, attitudes, and values of the people who create this material.

Zito also suggests that we can, perhaps, make inferences about the people who partake of the mass media—though there is a good deal of controversy about how much we can know about those who consume the mass media. Content analysis is an indirect way of making inferences about people. Instead of asking them questions, we examine what they read or watch and work backward, assuming that what people read and watch are good reflections of their attitudes, values, and so on. We know that people interpret television programs in different ways, depending upon their backgrounds and education—so we cannot assume that everyone interprets (that is, responds to the content in) a given television show or movie the same way.

Generally speaking, when we do a content analysis, we try to obtain a substantial amount of material to examine, and we always do it from a comparative point of view. The crucial decision we must make is which categories to examine. For example, consider the matter of violence on television. If we are to examine violent content, we have to define what we mean by *violence*, decide whether "comic" violence is violence, when "insults" are violence, and whether accidents resulting in bodily harm are violence.

We would also want to know how much violence there is, relatively speaking, on television. For example, a content analysis of the amount of violence on television (or in the comics) at any given moment or period in time is not as useful as a content analysis that compares the amount of violence on television (or in the comics) at a given moment with the amount found 10 or 20 years ago. One reason we conduct content analysis is to determine whether or not there have been interesting changes over the years. We are looking for trends in such instances.

Content analysis might also be used to compare and contrast two different television programs (or two different kinds of programs) in the United States, or to compare television content across different countries. Sometimes we might focus our attention on such phenomena as basic values and attitudes, most important roles for men or women, or allusions to political or social matters found in a given television series or kind of program or comic strip or magazine. In all cases, however, we must quantify our findings—that is, deal with some element that can be counted.

Problems in Conducting Content Analysis

There is a basic assumption implicit in content analyses, namely, that an investigation of messages and communication gives insights into the people who create the messages and communication. These materials, we assume, provide vicarious experiences, inform, reinforce values and beliefs, and offer a variety of uses and gratifications.

On the most immediate level, the matter of defining terms is critical. For example, how do we define *violence*? Researchers of violent content in the media have to offer their definitions of the term, and there is a great deal of disagreement among researchers about what violence is and how it should be defined. Is "intention" to commit harm violence? If so, we can expect to find a good deal more violence on television than if we limit our understanding of violence to actual physical harm. And what about attempts to commit harm that are unsuccessful? What about verbal abuse? Is that violence?

What most researchers do is offer "operational definitions" of concepts or subjects they are investigating—definitions that contain a description of how the concept is to be measured or counted. In the case of violence, for instance, we could say that (for the purpose of a content analysis) violence will be taken to cover "actions and threats involving bodily harm done purposefully." It is often necessary to write rather involved operational definitions of terms or concepts being used in a content analysis. In the example just given, the notion of purpose is mentioned. That means that accidental harm or injury done to a person is not considered violence. And what about comic violence? Is slapstick to be considered violence? Clearly, if you define violence very narrowly, you will find little of it in any sample you examine; if you define it very broadly, you will find it everywhere. Where do you draw the line?

Another problem involves finding a "measurable unit," some standard way of analyzing your material. In doing a content analysis of a comic strip, it is reasonable to consider the frame as the standard unit. If you have a page with 10 strips on it and 4 frames in each strip, you have 40 frames to analyze. If you are doing a content analysis of newspaper articles, you can use something like column inches, as long as the columns are the same widths. If they are not, you have to make allowance for this, by counting the actual areas in terms of square inches. But what do you do about television? Generally speaking, television researchers have used time units as their standard measure, and have investigated such things as the number of violent incidents per hour (after having defined violence operationally).

If you do not have a uniform standard measure that is easily quantified, your data (and remember, content analysis is a quantitative technique) will not be worth very much, because comparisons will be either impossible to make or meaningless. There is also the problem of "coder reliability." Will everyone watching a given television program and counting the amounts and kinds of violence come up with the same figures?

Advantages of Using Content Analysis

Content analysis is an inexpensive method of getting information about people. Using printed materials is inexpensive and relatively easy to do. Comics, for example, cost very little—and the same applies to magazines, newspapers, and other print media. Much of this material is available in libraries and on microfilm.

Content analysis also allows researchers to deal with subjects that are very current. They can work with the latest magazines or comic strips (and compare them with earlier ones), which means researchers can keep their fingers on the collective pulse, so to speak, and study phenomena as they develop—fads, fashions, crazes, and social movements.

If you have a decent library to use, you can also study the recent (and not-so-recent) past with considerable ease. This applies, particularly, to print media such as books, newspapers, and magazines. Many libraries have substantial collections of newspapers on microfilm, which means that obtaining material to subject to content analysis is not terribly difficult.

Content analysis is an unobtrusive method. One of the problems of doing research, we have discovered, is that the presence of researchers influences what they find. People act differently when they know (or even think) they are being observed. So content analysis is a way of avoiding the problem of researcher influence on individuals. But we cannot completely escape the impact of the researcher on research design. As Gideon Sjoberg and Roger Nett point out in *A Methodology for Social Research* (1968):

> The researcher himself is a variable in the research design. He influences the course of any research he undertakes, and his actions are in turn structured by the broader society in which he lives. (pp. 2-3)

The implications of this statement are that even in content analysis, which is an unobtrusive method, the interests, beliefs, and maybe even the personalities of researchers are important, for these factors may play a role in determining what researchers choose to investigate. There is no escaping researcher influence, but in content analysis it is not direct, because mediated communication is being studied and not the behavior of people.

Finally, content analysis provides numbers. The technique is based on counting and/or measuring, and the findings are given in numerical form. Others can replicate the research and see whether or not they get the same numbers. If the content analysis was done correctly and the figures are accurate, the replicated study should obtain the same figures. But that is only part of the story, because once you have data, you have the problem of interpreting them.

Disadvantages of Using Content Analysis

There is always a problem with sampling: How representative is the material one studies relative to all the material that could be studied? To get around this problem, content analysts often study a sizable amount of material. But what is the right amount of material to study and how do you determine a reasonable way of sampling this material? For instance, how many hours of television should be sampled to determine, with any degree of accuracy, how much violence there is on television? We usually get around this problem by selecting certain kinds of television programming that we consider particularly important—children's television, prime-time network television, and so on.

How do we know that what researchers "find" in the material they analyze is what the creators of the material being analyzed "put" into it? This matter was alluded to earlier. At one time, communications researchers assumed that television viewers, for instance, were affected by (and tended to interpret) a given program the same way. This was known as the "magic bullet" theory. It is described by Shearon Lowery and Melvin DeFleur in *Milestones in Mass Communication Research: Media Effects* (1983) as follows: "Early thinking about propaganda was that, like magic bullets, it struck all members of the mass audience equally and created uniform effects among them in a very direct way" (p. 105). We now agree that people respond differently to the mass media and are not hit by magic bullets. People have different interests, educations, personalities, and backgrounds, and all of these factors play roles in how they respond to mass media.

The recent development of "reader response" theories suggests that "readers" (consumers of media) play a very important role in making sense of the media. Some theorists have even argued that readers play as important a role in finding meaning in media as "creators" do in making material carried by the media. The point of all this is that we must be careful not to assume too much when we analyze our findings.

Content Analysis Project:
Newspaper Comics Pages

This research project has been designed to make it possible for all students to undertake original research and obtain numerical and other data that they can then interpret. In certain cases, content analyses can be difficult to conduct, especially when one is dealing with attitudes and beliefs or other topics that are difficult to define with precision. It also occurs with topics that do not easily lend themselves to measurable units that are easy to work with. To avoid these problems, this project uses the comics pages in newspapers.

The purpose of our content analysis will be to see whether or not (and, if so, how) comics have changed over the years and what comics may reflect about changes in American culture and society. We will consider such things as the amount and kind of violence in them, the number of men and women in them, the number of words "spoken" by men and by women in them, allusions to social and political events in them, social and racial characteristics of the characters, and attitudes and values found in the strips. (These categories form several concepts or constructs that will be used later in answering the research questions and in interpreting the findings.)

This exercise is similar in nature to the kind of research a scholar might undertake, except that it is much smaller in scale. It also will present you with a number of problems or dilemmas to deal with as you undertake the research.

Figure 3.1 shows a sample comic strip frame and lists some things to consider in decoding the elements in comics. Figure 3.2 provides a chart that can be used for the analysis or as an example that can be adapted to your particular purposes.

Carrying Out the Content Analysis

(1) Use a recent comics page from a local or regional newspaper. Cut it out of the newspaper and save it. This should be a page from a Monday-through-Saturday edition.

(2) Using the same newspaper, obtain comics pages from 20 or 40 years ago (or 30 or 60 years ago, or whatever your instructor suggests) to compare with the comics page you have on hand. You can photocopy microfilm pages or do the research at a microfilm machine. These pages should be from approximately the same time of year—that is, if you selected a page from your newspaper during the first week in October, you should find copies of earlier comics pages from the first week in October.

If your instructor assigns different students different years to study, your class can cover a wide period of time. Since the comics have been around for 90 years, as a class you can get a

(1) speech in regular balloons
(2) thoughts in scalloped balloons
(3) sound effects in zigzagged balloons
(4) facial expressions
(5) lines to indicate movement
(6) panel for continuity
(7) setting
(8) art styles—light and dark, composition, and so on
(9) language—meanings of words and punctuation
(10) clothes, objects, and other examples of material culture

Figure 3.1. Decoding a Comic Strip Frame

considerable amount of data on how newspaper comics have evolved. Several students can be assigned the same date and year, also. This is always interesting because frequently they end up with different statistics on everything from the number of frames on a page to the number of characters found in a strip.

(3) Count the number of strips on each page, the number of frames on each page, the number of male and female characters on each page, the number of words male and female characters speak on each page, and the number of incidents of violence (and kinds of violence) on each page. In counting the number of male and female figures, each time you see a male or female figure in a frame, count it. Suppose you have a strip with four

19__	19__	Subject
		number of strips on page
		total number of frames on page
		total number of characters (male and female)
		number of male characters
		percentage male characters
		number of female characters
		percentage of female characters
		total number of words spoken by all characters
		number of words spoken by male characters
		percentage of words spoken by male characters
		number of words spoken by female characters
		percentage of words spoken by female characters
		total number of violent incidents per page
		percentage of violent frames per page
		references to politics, societal problems, and so on
		other matters of interest:

Figure 3.2. Newspaper Comics Pages Content Analysis Chart

frames and the same male character appears in all four frames. For content analysis purposes, that constitutes four male representations. Each time a male or female character appears, it is counted.

(4) Determine the percentage of male and female figures, the percentage of words spoken by male and female figures, and the percentage of frames with violence in them.

(5) Figure out a way to deal with the social characteristics of the characters other than sex—age, race, or whatever—to the extent this is possible, and with allusions to social and political events, values, attitudes, and related concerns. Do you find patterns of dominance and submission? Are there interesting attitudes toward authority that you find? Are the differences in

the kinds of violence you find ("serious" versus "comic") significant? How do you distinguish between them? Have there been significant changes in the kinds of strips found on the pages? If so, what are they? Why do you think they have occurred? How would you classify the strips on your two pages? Here, you must find classification systems that cover all the strips and whose categories are mutually exclusive.

(6) List the problems you faced in making your content analysis and explain how you dealt with them. For example, how did you define *comic strip*, and how did you distinguish comic strips from cartoons that may also have been on the same page? How did you deal with animals in the counts you made?

(7) Write an essay dealing with your findings and with the inferences or conclusions you came to based on your content analysis. This is an interpretative effort; it forces you to go beyond your data to try to figure out what your data on the changes in newspaper comics pages tell you about American culture and society. You should be able to use your statistics and other data to support your interpretations. Do not make things up—interpretation is not the same thing as invention.

While this exercise simulates actual content analysis research, it makes no effort to sample the comics systematically, which affects the generalizability of the results.

Writing a Report on the Findings of Your Content Analysis

(1) Write a brief introduction in which you give readers some background on the subject you investigated. Tell them what you wanted to find out, why you made your study, why it is important, and how you carried out your analysis. In writing this kind of a paper, you usually tell readers what you found at the beginning and then show them how you arrived at your conclusions. A research article is not structured like a mystery story, in which you find out the secrets at the very end.

(2) Be careful to offer operational definitions of all important terms or concepts and to explain why the unit of measurement you used makes sense. That is, go into some detail on the technical aspects of the content analysis.

(3) Present your findings in an easy-to-grasp manner—perhaps in some kind of table that makes your findings clear. In this exercise, it is useful to attach the comics pages you analyzed so readers can check on your findings. You will have to figure out how to classify the strips on each of your comics pages in some meaningful way.

(4) Offer some hypotheses about what your results suggest. How do the two pages of newspaper comic strips reflect American culture and society? What effects do you think the comics have on readers? This kind of writing is speculative, but it is based on "hard" data—the statistics you have compiled.

Do not be put off by the fact that you must make inferences; this is always a problem when interpreting data. One way to deal with this problem is by qualifying your conclusions. You can write that your findings "would seem to indicate" or "suggest" a conclusion rather than stating that your findings "prove" some conclusion (which they likely do not). It is a good idea to avoid *all* and *every* statements, which suggest certainty. Also, avoid the word *proof*. It has been suggested that nothing in social scientific research is ever proven, nor do social scientists set out to prove anything.

(5) Remember, also, to deal with problems you had in making the analysis and explain how you dealt with them. For example, were certain racial and ethnic groups excluded or underrepresented in the comics you studied? How did you deal with allusions to social and political matters? What did you do about animals in strips? How did you decide on a classification system that was revealing (as opposed to one such as "humorous" and "serious," which doesn't tell us very much).

Content analysis is one of the more important techniques used in research concerning the mass media. The content analysis you have conducted is a smaller-scale version of the kind that research scholars do, and the problems and difficulties you faced are similar in nature to those that they face. There are many kinds of content analyses and many problems involved in conducting them. What you have done in your analysis of newspaper comics pages is "real" research, however. It is my hope that this exercise has intrigued you and whetted your appetite for doing other kinds of research, some of which are explained in the chapters that follow.

Opinion surveys are often dubious indicators of actual behavior because they do not, and perhaps cannot, measure the seething, changing, character of the public temper. They generally fail to embody the rich context of motivation and cross-communication out of which opinions arise and activate people in the mass. . . . The paradox of scientific method is that we change phenomena by measuring them. The confrontation of interviewer and respondent forces the crystallization and expression of opinions where there were no more than chaotic swirls of thought. The respondent's statements themselves represent a form of behavior; they are commitments. A question asked by an interviewer changes an abstract and perhaps irrelevant matter into a genuine subject of action; the respondent confronts a voting decision, exactly as he might on the choice of candidates or on a proposition in a plebiscite. The conventional poll forces expression into predetermined channels, by presenting clear-cut and mutually exclusive choices. To accommodate one's thoughts to these channels represents for the respondent an arousal of interest, an affirmative act.

Leo Bogart, *Polls and the Awareness of Public Opinion* (1985, pp. 17-18)

4

Survey Interviews: Media Utilization

Surveys (in which a researcher asks people questions and fills out some form) and questionnaires (forms that are sent to people for them to fill out) are two of the most common ways of finding out what people think about things: their beliefs, their opinions, actions they've taken, actions they are contemplating, and so on. This is an example of descriptive research, designed to find out such things as what products people use, how they intend to vote in forthcoming elections, or their position on some social or political issue. There are other kinds of interviewing that can be done, such as depth interviewing, which will be discussed in Chapter 6.

Surveys must be distinguished from experiments, which are another way of finding information. As Julian L. Simon writes in *Basic Research Methods in Social Science: The Art of Empirical Investigation* (1969):

> A survey gathers data about variables *as they are found in the world.* The survey can *observe behavior,* as for example whether or not people are athletes, whether or not they smoke, whether or not the money supply is high some years, and whether or not there is prosperity in those years. The survey can also collect data on what people *say;* for example, researchers can ask people of various backgrounds for whom they will vote or how much liquor they drink. The important distinction between the survey and the experiment is that the survey takes the world as it comes, without trying to alter it, whereas the experiment systematically alters some aspects of the world in order to see what changes follow. (p. 229)

In the exercise described below you will construct an *instrument* (a social science term for a list of questions) and will use it to find out how much time people spend with the mass media—watching television, listening to the radio and records—and why they spend time with the media.

One thing you must do when conducting survey research is find the "right" people to interview. If you want to know how students are going to vote in an upcoming elections, you must find students who are eligible to vote. If you want to know how suburban housewives feel about some television program, you must get a representative sampling of suburban housewives. This is not always easy to do.

You must be concerned, then, with two factors. First, you must consider the social and economic characteristics of your respondents (the people you will be interviewing): age, sex, race, religion, education, and occupation, among other things. Second, you must ask questions that will provide useful information on the subject of your inquiry. Then, if you are lucky, you may be able to find correlations—that is, relationships—between, for example, occupation and voting intentions or education and magazines subscribed to.

As Rubin, Rubin, and Piele write in *Communication Research: Strategies and Sources* (1990): "Survey research often employs a correlational design, not looking for cause-and-effect connections but seeking to describe the opinions or attitudes of certain groups, or the relationships between two or more factors" (p. 178). Correlations may not tell us why something occurs (that is, what caused it)—though they can, in certain circumstances—but they still can provide interesting material about relationships. When relationships are established, we find, for example, that young people don't like talk shows, that senior citizens do like talk shows, and so on. This information is useful to people who wish to advertise products that appeal to young people or senior citizens.

One must be careful, however, because sometimes correlations don't always work out. For example, a television station in San Francisco had research data that viewers of *The Cosby Show* tended to watch a good deal of television news. So the station bought rights to rerun *Cosby* (at great expense), and then found that its audience didn't like watching the reruns in the late afternoon, when they were originally scheduled (just before the evening news), nor did they watch the show when it was rescheduled after the 11:00 p.m. news. As a result of this experience, the station lost a number of its regular news viewers and a great deal of money.

Problems with Surveys

When conducting survey research, you must define the topic you wish to investigate very carefully and precisely, since your topic will determine the questions you ask. That is, you must have a focus. Suppose, for example, you want to obtain information for a politician running for office. You may want to find out how different groups perceive the candidate. Is there a difference between the way men and women feel about the candidate and the candidate's various policies? How do middle-aged and older people view the candidate? White people and people of color? Once you obtain this information, the candidate can either modify or explain more clearly his or her policies.

You must figure out how to obtain a representative sampling of the social groups you want to survey. This is an important problem, because if you don't survey a representative sampling of your *population* (the technical term for a complete group of interest) your answers won't be worth very much. In the case of surveys made by professional polling organizations, relatively accurate information about the American public, some 250 million people, can be obtained by interviewing as few as 1,500 people. How can you possibly know what 250 million people think by asking only 1,500 people? The answer is that these professional polling organizations use carefully selected representative samples that accurately reflect characteristics of the general population. This "magic" is based on probability theory. The basic idea is that error is always present when using samples. The magnitude, or size, of the error is reduced, however, as the sample size increases—but only up to a point.

An Example

Let me offer an example that is oversimplified, but shows you how this works. Consider the figure below, composed of 15 squares. If you know what a couple of squares are like, you know what all the other squares are like.

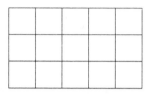

In survey research, the "figure" is more complicated, but if you can find a representative sample of a certain size (based on obtaining random samples of a size that statisticians say is necessary) you can often obtain relatively accurate information—to within 3% one way or the other, and sometimes even less. According to statisticians, a sample that was twice or even 10 times as large as the typical 1,500 people would not be much more accurate.

We will assume (to simplify matters) that the sampling of people you use in doing your survey will be random and representative. You can try to find as many different kinds of people to interview as you can, to help things along, but a random sample is not necessary for this exercise.

Advantages of Surveys

Conducting surveys is a relatively inexpensive way of obtaining information. You can ask a considerable number of questions, though you must be careful that you don't ask so many that your respondents, the people answering your questions, become irritated.

If the sampling is correct, surveys and other forms of opinion polls are generally reasonably accurate. Pollsters have become very sophisticated in obtaining representative samples of people and all kinds of information.

Information can be obtained on past behavior and on future behavior (voting intentions, potential purchases, opinions on issues) that is useful to the parties doing or paying for the surveys. As mentioned earlier, as in the case of the San Francisco television station that purchased *Cosby* reruns, sometimes this information can lead one astray. We sometimes make unwarranted inferences from the information we obtain.

Answers to surveys can be presented in numerical form and subjected to various kinds of analysis. Once information about the social characteristics of the respondents is obtained, it can be used to make many correlations and to predict behavior in the general public. We see this during elections. Television networks and stations employ pollsters who have developed sophisticated ways of sampling people as they leave voting booths. As a result of information obtained from these people (and based on the representativeness of certain districts), very often election outcomes can be determined even before voting has stopped. This has now become a big issue the media and politicians are wrestling with, since many feel that the process may affect elections by dissuading people who have not voted from voting.

Disadvantages of Surveys

In conducting survey research, getting a representative sampling is often difficult and can be very expensive. This is not a concern we have to worry about in this exercise, however.

Also, because surveys must have some focus, they must be limited in scope. The list of questions must be fixed, and there is no room for maneuver, as in the depth interview.

People answering surveys may not give honest answers, if, for example, they fear that they won't look good or the surveyor will have a negative opinion of them. This is particularly true where controversial issues are concerned; questionnaires are often a better choice in such situations. In answering survey questions, people often exaggerate their incomes, have mistaken notions of what social class they belong to, lie about their ages, and claim to have voted for the winner in elections (because they want to be on the "winning" side). They may also not really understand a question, but think they do. All these factors affect a study's validity and accuracy.

In real life, you should always find out whether the survey you propose to do has already been done recently. If this is the case, there is no need to duplicate the survey. Also, it is a good idea to pretest the survey, to find out whether some of the questions confuse people, whether some of the questions are ambiguous or too personal, and whether there are any other problems with your questions.

Survey Interview Assignment: Media Usage Among Students

In this exercise, you want to find out how many hours, in a typical day, the students you survey spend watching television or VCRs, listening to the radio or their records, and reading newspapers, magazines, or books. It will be interesting to see, for example, how grade point average, age, sex, socioeconomic class, and other social characteristics correlate with media usage patterns.

We actually have a good deal of information, taken from national surveys, on this subject. It will be interesting for you to compare your findings with the figures for the country as a whole.

Constructing a Survey

Constructing a survey is difficult because all your questions must be unambiguous and perfectly clear to everyone, otherwise respondents will not be able to answer them correctly. Here are some considerations to keep in mind when writing your survey on media usage:

(1) *The order of the questions:* Do you ask "interesting" questions first, so your respondent will answer them, or do you start off asking questions about your respondent's social characteristics?

(2) *The logic of the question order:* Some questions logically come before others. For example, you can't ask people for their

opinion about something until you find out, first, whether or not they know anything about it.

(3) *The utility of the questions:* You have only a limited number of questions you can ask (to avoid irritating your respondent), so you must ask questions that give you the information you need.

(4) *How many questions to ask:* Is one question enough or are several needed? Each question must be limited to one topic. This means, in some cases, you must ask a number of related questions to obtain all the information you want. Never put two topics into one question.

(5) *The respondent's ability to answer:* Will the respondent have the necessary information to answer your questions?

(6) *The content of the questions:* Are any of the questions biased in some way? That is, have you, without being aware of it, "loaded" some of the questions so that certain answers will be given? Remember, *how* you ask a question plays an important role in what answers you get. To the extent that it is possible, your questions should be neutral. Your task is to get other people's opinions, not to get them to agree with yours.

(7) *The language used in the questions:* Are the questions worded clearly? Are all terms explained so the respondent understands everything? Some respondents may be shy or may feel that asking you questions about the meanings of certain terms will suggest that they are ignorant, and thus will give you answers to questions that they don't understand.

(8) *The forms of the questions:* Which kinds of questions do you wish to ask? If you ask *open* questions, so respondents can give lengthy answers, it is difficult to quantify what you find. If you ask *closed* questions, in which respondents select from choices you offer them, you may be oversimplifying things and not getting people's real opinions.

(9) *The purposes of the questions:* Do you wish to measure intensity—how strongly people feel about issues—as well as opinions and beliefs and attitudes? If so, how do you do this?

(10) *The clarity of the questions:* Have you created any "double-barreled" questions by mistake? These questions require a single answer although they ask several questions—for example, "How satisfied are you with television coverage of Europe and the Middle East?" The respondent cannot separate coverage of Europe from coverage of the Middle East in his or her reply.

Constructing a Survey Interview Instrument

For this exercise, construct an instrument that obtains information about how much time your respondents spend listening to or watching (or involved with) various media and how they feel about and use the different media. Some things you might want to investigate include the following:

(1) What do they own in the way of color or black-and-white television sets, VCRs, stereos, compact disc players, boom boxes, radios, and so on? What do their families have at home?

(2) How much time do they spend listening to or watching each of the various media? When do they partake of the different media?

(3) Do they do other things while involved with the media? Do they listen to the radio or watch television while they do homework or chores around the house?

(4) How do they use the media? To kill time? To entertain themselves? To relax? To find out what's going on in the world? To socialize with their friends? To deal with loneliness or stress?

(5) What are their favorite radio stations and programs, television shows, magazines, and the like?

Be on the lookout for poor questions. If the answers you get are confused, if you get many respondents saying they "don't know" or "don't understand," or refusing to answer a question, something is wrong. You should try to obtain material that is specific. Thus you should find out how many minutes or hours your respondents spend with each of the media and when they tend to spend time with them.

Interpreting Your Findings

It would be best if you could interview 10 people about their media usage, trying to get as representative a sample as possible. If you want to find out about media usage among college students, for example, it would be good to interview two students from each of the various classes: freshmen, sophomores, juniors, seniors, and graduate students. You could narrow your focus further, and interview members of your research class or some other class.

When you have finished your interviewing, consider how you might best present your findings: Can you create a chart that will show what you have found? Whatever the case, you should assemble your data in some logical way and then try to figure out what your data mean. What do they suggest about the group you studied?

Writing a Report on
Your Findings from the Survey

(1) Write a brief introduction telling what information you wanted to find, why you wanted to obtain this information, and what you found. Remember, the conclusions come at the beginning of your paper, not at the end.

(2) Attach a copy of your survey so readers can evaluate it in terms of its fairness and comprehensiveness.

(3) Present your data in some easy-to-read format, giving the questions and the results of your survey. Make sure you connect your findings with social characteristics of the people you studied.

(4) Discuss the results of your survey and the conclusions you draw from the survey. Remember to qualify your answers and avoid sweeping generalizations.

(5) Deal with difficulties you faced in making the survey and explain what you did to overcome or compensate for them.

In . . . most . . . usages, the following elements appear in the definition of role: it provides a *strategy* for coping with a recurrent type of situation; it is *socially identified,* more or less clearly, as an entity; it is subject to being played recognizably by *different individuals;* and it supplies a major basis for *identifying* and *placing* persons in society.

Ralph Turner, "Role: Sociological Aspects," in
International Encyclopedia of the Social Sciences,
Volume 13 (1968, p. 552)

5

Social Roles: Television Soap Opera Characters

The concept of "social role" comes from social psychology and means, in everyday language, the behavior that is expected of people, given their place in some group or organization. A role is generally understood to mean a persistent pattern of conduct that is always connected with a particular situation. The term "role" comes from the theater, where it means a part in a play.

When we look at the way people behave in terms of their roles, it suggests that we are adopting a theatrical or dramatic point of view; we see life as being like a play in which everyone is playing roles (and not necessarily being or revealing themselves). Sociologists who adopt this perspective sometimes call it a "dramatistic metaphor." This metaphor suggests that much of our behavior can be seen as a kind of acting for the benefit of others with whom we are involved, our "audience." We can look at people's behavior, then, in terms of the various roles they assume in the conduct of their daily lives. They are not necessarily conscious that they are adopting these roles because the behavior patterns have become internalized and seem completely natural.

Factors Involved in Role Analysis

There are, then, two factors to focus our attention upon: One is society, groups, and organizations, and the other is behavior. Society, in general, and groups and organizations, in particular, have a great deal of influence on the way people act. One of the basic functions of our educational system and family life is to teach children how to play roles properly. Society functions much more smoothly when people know what roles they are to play and how to play them than when there is confusion about roles.

We realize, also, that a given person may play many different roles during a typical day. Jane Q. Public might typically play the roles of parent (to her children), wife (to her husband), professor (to her students), administrator (to her colleagues), writer (to an editor), and so on. Roles are typically differentiated from status, which involves the amount of prestige and power one has in society or in some organization. Of course, the status one has affects the roles one plays.

Final Definition of Social Role

If we put all of the matters considered above together, we arrive at our final definition of social role: *persistent patterns of conduct and behavior that are connected to the individual's position in some social structure or organization.* A social role can be thought of as being a link between a person's personality structure and the social structure (see Exhibit 5.1). Our parents generally spend a good deal of time teaching us how to play various roles.

Another method we have of learning roles is by observing "models," people we respect and admire, and imitating them in various ways. The importance of heroes and heroines (especially in the mass media) cannot be underestimated here. Most Americans watch about three hours of television a day and spend a considerable amount of time listening to records and watching films or videos, which means that we are exposed to large numbers of heroes, heroines, and other kinds of characters with whom we identify to varying degrees and in varying ways. One of the most important things roles do for people is help them attain *identities.*

Exhibit 5.1

Collective representations are the result of an immense co-operation, which stretches not only into space but into time as well; to make them, a multitude of minds have associated, united and combined their ideas and sentiments; for them, long generations have accumulated their experience and their knowledge. A special intellectual activity is therefore concentrated in them which is infinitely richer and complexer than that of the individual. From that one can understand how the reason has been able to go beyond the limits of empirical knowledge. It does not owe this to any vague, mysterious virtue but simply to the fact that according to the well-known formula, man is double. There are two beings in him: an individual being which has its foundation in the organism and the circle of whose activities is therefore strictly limited, and a social being which represents the highest reality in the intellectual and moral order that we can know by observation—I mean society. This duality of our nature has as its consequence in the practical order, the irreducibility of a moral ideal to a utilitarian motive, and in the order of thought, the irreducibility of reason to individual experience. In so far as he belongs to society, the individual transcends himself, both when he thinks and when he acts.

SOURCE: Durkheim (1965, p. 29).

Significant Others and Identity

When we play roles we need others to respond to them in the correct manner—that is, in the way we intend our roles to be perceived. A famous social psychologist, George Herbert Mead, used the term "significant others" to describe the people who respond to us and help us confirm our identities.

In *Sociology: A Biographical Approach*, Peter L. Berger and Brigitte Berger (1972) write:

The socialized part of the self is commonly called *identity*. Every society may be viewed as holding a repertoire of identities—little

boy, little girl, father, mother, policeman, professor, thief, archbishop, general and so forth. By a kind of invisible lottery, these
identities are assigned to different individuals. Some of them are
assigned from birth, such as little boy or little girl. Others are
assigned later in life, such as clever little boy or pretty little girl
(or, conversely, stupid little boy or ugly little girl). Other identities
are put up, as it were, for subscription, and individuals may obtain
them by deliberate effort, such as policeman or archbishop. But
whether an identity is assigned or achieved, in each case it is
appropriated by the individual through a process of interaction
with others. It is others who identify him in a specific way. Only
if an identity is confirmed by others is it possible for that identity
to be real to the individual holding it. (p. 62)

Roles, then, when they are confirmed by significant others, help
confer identity.

Social Role and
Counterrole Analysis of Soap Operas

The purpose of your research into social roles is to determine
what kinds of roles are assigned to men and women in a sampling of some representative soap operas. What roles are em-
phasized and what roles are deemphasized for men, women,
African-Americans, aged people, ethnic minorities, children,
adolescents, and others? To carry out this assignment you
should consider some of the following matters:

(1) the occupation of a character or the position a character has in
    some organization or group
(2) the status a character has, which is tied to his or her position
(3) counterroles of various characters (such as doctor-patient, clerk-
    customer) that complement particular roles
(4) privileges and obligations connected to a given role (e.g., privi-
    leges and obligations of the head of a corporation versus those
    of a clerk-typist who works in the office pool of that organization)
(5) perceptions of roles—how people's roles are envisioned in given
    situations and what these roles are as seen by others

(6) performance of roles—how various characters perform their roles and how these performances are seen by others
(7) conflicting roles—what happens when a character is torn between two different roles, when performing one role will interfere with performing the other
(8) relations between roles and people's values, beliefs, and attitudes
(9) role props—devices (clothes, hairstyles, language, eyeglasses, settings, and so on) used to define characters' roles

You should be aware of these aspects of roles when you make your social role analysis of the television programs.

Roles played by people require others, acting in counterroles, to succeed. These roles and counterroles form what we might call a "scene" (and what you observe on television, when you watch your soap operas, will actually or technically be scenes). Figure 5.1 shows the roles and counterroles of a professor. As you can imagine, a professor plays different kinds of professional roles, depending upon whether he or she is speaking with the president of the university, a student, a colleague (who may have higher rank), or staff people—secretaries, librarians, or technicians.

In carrying out your research, be sure to use a soap opera that has interesting characters who function as socially significant role models. After you describe the roles and counterroles of the characters you have dealt with, you should relate what you have found to society in general and the social concerns most people have. You should speculate, for example, how these role models may be influencing people or may have influenced people. You might also want to say something about whether the heroes and heroines you have studied reflect basic American values and norms or something else.

Problems in Social Role Analysis

Focusing upon social roles suggests that society is rather static. In static societies, people are awarded their status and roles by ascription (based on their families and connections)

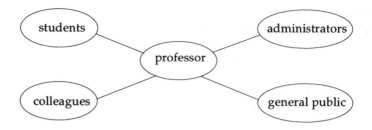

Figure 5.1. Roles and Counterroles of a Professor

rather than "achieving" roles and status (on the basis of hard work). In most modern societies, however, things are rather fluid and people change roles and identities from time to time— sometimes, constantly.

Focusing upon social roles tends to neglect other aspects of life—people's personalities, their values, their intelligence, their character, and their moral sensibilities. This means we must be careful not to assume that social roles are the only important thing to know about people.

Since people vary their roles during a given day—professor, wife, mother, consultant—depending upon the situations in which they find themselves, we must be sure we don't distort things by neglecting certain roles and focusing on atypical roles.

Advantages of Social Role Analysis

Observing social roles in television soap operas is inexpensive, and the material is easy to find and record. In addition, the genre is an important one. There is a good deal of research by scholars on this subject—in books and articles in scholarly journals—that you can use as background for your work.

Social role analysis offers insights into how society maintains itself. All societies provide people with a repertoire of social roles, which people frequently internalize and don't even recognize. These roles are connected with basic attitudes and values, so a study of social roles provides a useful means of obtaining insights about American society. Consider dealing with some or all of the following topics:

(1) demographics of characters: age, sex, occupation, education, race, ethnicity, socioeconomic class (to the extent you can determine these)
(2) attitudes toward authority, members of the opposite sex, the family, work, power, racial minorities, ethnic minorities, and so on
(3) basic goals, basic values, and beliefs of characters
(4) moral sensibilities of each of the characters
(5) life-styles of the characters and what these imply

Since social roles as reflected in the mass media often function as "models" for people, who learn how individuals behave in various roles (so social learning theory suggests), studying social roles helps us find out how people see themselves, or, to be more accurate, how they are being taught to see themselves. For example, consider the roles given to women in soap operas. A great deal of the time, women are turned into "sex objects"; they are seldom shown in high-status occupations, are often portrayed as silly (though sometimes vicious), and generally do not provide satisfactory role models to the millions of women who watch (or for men either, who get ideas from such portrayals about how women should be treated). One of the basic goals of the women's liberation movement has been to change the way women are portrayed in soap operas and other television programs, since the old roles provide unsuitable models for young and old people of both sexes.

Disadvantages of Social Role Analysis

It is often difficult to determine accurately certain demographic aspects of the various characters in soap operas. We may know something about their occupations and can infer other things about them from this, but we can't be certain. This is true in real life as well.

Also, soap operas have been on television so long that it is difficult to know what sample to use that is truly representative.

And the actions of soap opera characters are often so exaggerated and the characters so unusual that analyzing their role relationships may not provide insights about the roles and counterroles of ordinary people.

Social Role Analysis Assignment

Analyze the roles and counterroles of the main characters in a reasonable sample of daily or evening soap operas and construct diagrams (as many as needed) showing important roles and counterroles. Pay particular attention to the roles given female characters, how the characters established their identities in the story, and how they used other characters to affirm these identities. Utilize the list of topics for consideration found in the discussion of advantages of social role analysis.

Writing a Report on
Your Role Analysis Research

(1) Write an introduction giving your reader some background on the subject. Deal with research by others on soap operas as a means of establishing a sense of context. Then, tell what conclusions you came to after you made your study.

(2) Discuss the roles you observed and how you conducted your research. How many programs did you study? How many hours of television did you watch? Which roles, or aspects of roles, did you focus on? Why? What problems did you face in making your analysis? How did you solve them? You might also say something about various props (clothes, houses, cars, hairstyles, objects of one sort or another) characters used to give others (including viewers) a sense of their roles and identities.

(3) Make a diagram of the important roles and counterroles you studied. You might offer brief descriptions of the plots of the episodes you studied, so readers get a sense of things and your role diagrams make more sense.

(4) Tie your research to findings by others about soap operas in general and your soap opera in particular. Many articles about soap operas have appeared in the *Journal of Communication* and other scholarly journals, and there are also books on

soap operas such as *Dallas* and its worldwide audience, and soap operas in general. You should say something about how your findings relate to work done by scholars in this area. One interesting question to consider is whether or not the roles of women have changed in significant ways over the last decade or so in soap operas and in the mass media in general. Depending upon how much time you have, you might also investigate work by sociologists and other social scientists on role model theory in general.

Be alert to the kind of information your informant is conveying to you. Is it his or her analysis of the topic or a pure description of it? Is this the informant's perspective or that of someone else? Is your informant being honest, or manipulating the material to impress you (are there ulterior motives involved)? Anytime there is a sense of discomfort in the atmosphere, try to pinpoint its cause. . . . When you have located an appropriate informant, one who is cooperative, knowledgeable, and reliable, there are various considerations for the interview itself. The place where the interview is to occur must be selected carefully. It should be convenient both to researcher and informant. It should not be too noisy, because the ethnographer must pay close attention to the interview, and of the requirements of tape recording, if such is to be used.

Lebriz Tosuner-Fikes, "A Guide to Anthropological Fieldwork on Contemporary American Culture," in Conrad Phillip Kottak (Ed.), *Researching American Culture* (1982, pp. 27-28)

6

Depth Interviews: Favorite Singers and Records

In this research assignment, you will investigate people's favorite singers and records and try to find out why those people like certain singers and songs. You will do this by conducting depth interviews. A depth interview is really an extended conversation, but it has a different purpose from an ordinary conversation. In a typical conversation we talk about our work, our families, events in the news, people we know, and so on. The conversation can ramble and move in many different directions. The depth interview, on the other hand, is highly focused. It is conducted to get at matters such as hidden feelings or attitudes and beliefs that respondents may not be aware of or that are only dimly in their consciousness.

A depth interview is a kind of probe. When conducted by trained interviewers, many of whom have advanced degrees in psychology, depth interviews can sometimes last an hour or more. The reason these interviews take so much time is that it is necessary to penetrate the defenses people often put up to prevent their hidden beliefs from coming to light—defenses that they frequently are not conscious of and do not recognize in their behavior.

Depth interviewing is often done for commercial reasons—to find out why people purchase one brand of coffee and not another, how they feel about cake mixes, or why they use cigarette lighters. Ernest Dichter, the father of motivation research, has written a number of books that are full of what was discovered when depth interviews were conducted about various products—everything from fur coats to brands of soup.

Focus Groups and Oral Histories

Sometimes focus groups are used to find out a number of people's opinions about some product. This form of group interview is not the same as a depth interview; the information obtained in focus groups is more a matter of group opinions and attitudes than hidden beliefs. A focus group research assignment is presented in Chapter 9, where this form of interview will be discussed in more detail.

A modification of the depth interview, the oral history, can be done using a tape recorder. The aims of depth interviews and oral histories are vaguely similar, but in the oral history the focus is upon a person's experiences and what these experiences tell us about a period in history or the lives of the people giving their histories. With oral histories, the researcher tries to get details, recollections, and anecdotes (and, in some cases, songs and poems, folklore, and the like) that can give a personal perspective on history and the way people lived in earlier times.

Problems with Depth Interviews

You may have difficulty getting the right *respondents*—the right persons to interview—for your project. Some of the people you interview may be shy or may be otherwise reluctant (for various reasons) to talk freely with you, so you may not get the kind of information you are looking for. Some interviewees talk around any subject and are hard to pin down; others are afraid to express their feelings.

Also, it is sometimes difficult to maintain a depth interview long enough to gain any real answers. For this assignment, a 15- or 20-minute interview will do, but even that may be difficult to maintain.

You may not know precisely what it is you are looking for in your depth interviews, other than that you are trying to find out whether there are any hidden reasons that explain why people like the singers they do and buy the records they do. You probably won't know what you've found, also, until you have analyzed your notes from a number of depth interviews and discovered what, if anything, they reveal.

Advantages of Depth Interviews

You can collect a great deal of detailed information when you conduct depth interviews. You can ask follow-up questions and pursue topics that interest you for a considerable length of time.

In conducting such interviews, you often obtain unexpected information that other forms of research might not discover. Sigmund Freud argued that slips of the tongue and dreams people have can be used to obtain information about their mental states that other kinds of research cannot get at. He developed a method called "free association," in which his patients were asked to tell about their dreams and whatever else came into their heads. Depth interviewing can be seen as an adaptation of this technique. The more people talk, the more they reveal (give away) about themselves. In the depth interviewing you will do for this assignment, you will not be concerned with analyzing people, but with finding out why people like the singers they do and buy the records they do.

When conducting a depth interview, you can adapt to a situation. If a promising topic comes up you can pursue it. You can ask the respondent to be more specific, when this is useful, or to deal in generalizations, when this makes sense.

The topics being investigated in this assignment are of widespread interest. Many people have stereo systems and extensive record collections, and many people listen to the radio for hours at a time and follow the newest releases. The subject, then, is important to many young men and women and is one about which many of them will be happy to talk.

Disadvantages of Depth Interviews

It can be difficult to handle the enormous amounts of material that depth interviews can generate. It is possible to obtain a great deal of information during each interview, and if you conduct a number of such interviews, you can face formidable amounts of data.

If you use a tape recorder in your interviews, normally you would transcribe this material, a procedure that is very time-consuming. In this particular case, since this is a student research exercise, you will not be asked to transcribe your tapes.

Finally, it is not always possible for respondents to give meaningful answers in depth interviews. Moving from discussing *what* they did to *why* they did it is not easy for many people, especially since some people don't always know why they take certain actions. In this case, they may know what singers and records they like, but they might not know why they like them.

Depth Interview Research Project

The subject of your depth interview is the preferences people have for singers and records. Music is something that plays an important part in our lives and about which many people have strong and definite feelings and opinions. The goal of this research assignment is to find out *why* your respondents like certain singers and record albums. It is not to find out what they listen to in an average day, though this information may be useful. Your concern will be to get at feelings people have for singers and records, to see what they "mean" to people.

You will have to decide what this "meaning" is. There are all kinds of associations people make with singers and records, and you should try to find out what these associations are and what they signify. In essence, you will be fishing around, trying to find things that your respondents may not be aware of. Interview four to six people for this exercise, spending approximately 20 minutes with each person.

Carrying Out the Depth Interview

(1) If you can, make audiotapes of your interviews, so you have precise records of what was said. Also, take notes on important matters while you interview each person.

(2) Be on the lookout for feelings, opinions, and attitudes that people have, even if they seem irrelevant or trivial. What might

seem to be trivial may end up telling you a good deal. This means that when you interview people, you should ask questions that are open-ended and allow your respondents plenty of room to speculate, offer opinions, and so on.

(3) You should get some preliminary demographic information about your respondents, so you can see whether or not any correlations can be made between socioeconomic class, education, gender, or race and what you find. You should interview people who fall into a certain category and are alike in some important respect for this exercise. That means you have to figure out a way to find respondents who will have the attributes you want.

(4) Make a preliminary list of some questions you might want to ask to get the interview off to a good start and to get the information you want. In Robert L. Leon's *Psychiatric Interviewing: A Primer* (1988), he points out that people wait for clues—both verbal and nonverbal—that tell them how to respond when they are being interviewed. "Doctors, as well as patients, give clues of which they unaware" (p. 8), he points out. He then makes a distinction between directive and nondirective interviewing:

> We speak of two kinds of interviews, directive and nondirective. This refers to the interviewer's communications to the patient about how the interview will progress and whether the doctor or patient will determine what information will come from the interview. The terms "directive" and "nondirective" do not refer to the interview's purpose. Nondirective means allowing patients to open the interview, develop it, and proceed at their own pace. The doctor must let go yet still maintain control, which may sound paradoxical. (p. 17)

Leon's book was written for psychiatrists, so we must substitute "interviewer" and "interviewee" for "doctor" and "patient" here. The important thing is to let those being interviewed tell what's on their minds instead of falling into the mode of just answering questions that are asked of them. Leon makes a distinction between an interview and an interrogation (as carried on, say, by the police). When interviewing people, then, you must learn how to be a good listener and pick up on statements made and openings given you by interviewees. Ask questions that elicit further comments and opinions and explanations of statements interviewees make. And don't interrupt interviewees when they are telling you about their feelings and thoughts because you have some information you want to get.

What follows is a list of questions you might want to consider when doing a depth interview, after you have established rapport with your respondent and broken the ice:

- What is your favorite kind of music?
- What is it you like about it?
- How long have you liked it? Did you like something else before?
- What performers/singers/groups do you like the best?
- What is it about them that you like?
- Do you have many of their albums? How many? Which ones?
- What is your favorite album now? Any idea why?
- Do you have a favorite song now?
- Do you know the lyrics of the song?
- What do the lyrics mean to you?
- Anything special about the performance?
- How do you decide whether or not to buy an album?
- What albums have you bought recently?
- How often do you play them?
- What kind of feelings do you get when you listen to your favorite singer/song/album?
- Do you tend to listen to them at particular times, when you're in particular moods? If so, how would you describe your moods?
- Does the singer/song/album help you deal with any problems you have? If so, how?
- Do you ever buy albums because your friends do?
- Do you belong to any fan clubs? If so, for whom? If you were to join a fan club, which one would you join?
- What do you think is the most important thing about a song—the lyrics, the beat, the melody? Something else?
- If you could be switched into the body of some singer, which one would you choose?
- Have you ever been to any live performances in which you've seen singers or groups? If so, which ones? Which show did you like best?
- What's your favorite radio station? About how many hours a day/week do you listen to it? What kind of music does it play?

These are the kinds of questions you might consider asking. It would not be a good idea to bring this list of questions and ask them, one after another, because that would turn the depth interview into a survey. But you should consider questions that might lead your respondents to discuss their preferences in some detail.

There are a number of different kinds of responses an interviewer can make as an interview progresses:

- *understanding response:* Here you try to find out whether you understand what the respondent is telling you. You might ask for clarification of some kind. It is often useful to repeat something the interviewee has said in your question—"Did I understand you to say . . . ?"
- *probing response:* Here you try to obtain more information by asking follow-up questions and trying to get the respondent to discuss some point in more detail. You might ask how he or she feels about something, why he or she believes something, and so on.
- *evaluative response:* Here you offer a judgment of some kind about what your respondent has told you. In conducting your depth interviews, you should *avoid evaluative responses*, since your purpose is to obtain information, not to render judgments.
- *phatic response:* Here you just say something like "Uh huh" to indicate that you have heard the respondent and wish him or her to continue. This is a form of feedback that helps keep the interview moving. Conversations are actually structured, and respondents need to know that you have heard them and that they can continue talking.

(5) Be neutral. In conducting the interview, you should not offer any of your own opinions, since they might affect the answers you get. Do not evaluate your informant's statements and don't offer your own opinions about things. And don't ask "leading questions," questions that give the interviewee a hint of the answer you are looking for. Your job, remember, is to keep interviewees talking about themselves, their feelings, their attitudes, and related matters. You want to keep the conversation going and guide it, in as subtle a manner as possible, in the direction of the subject at hand. Say as little as possible, and

when you do speak, do so only to obtain more information from the interviewee.

Writing a Report on Your Depth Interview

(1) Write an introductory paragraph or two on the subject of your depth interview and why it is interesting and important.

(2) Describe your findings. What conclusions did you arrive at after your depth interviews? Where you able to discover anything interesting? Did your interviewees have any preferences in common? Did they use music in similar or different ways? Did you obtain any insights (which we will define as the discovery of interesting relationships between phenomena not previously known) from the interviews? Did you find anything that suggests that further research would be profitable?

(3) If you have found something that you think is interesting, use quotations and paraphrases from the interviews to support your contentions. It is always better to show results to your readers (via quotations) than to tell them (via something you say), especially if you have material that reveals hidden feelings and attitudes.

It may be, of course, that you found nothing interesting from your interviews. If that is the case, you should say so. You should not always expect to have research projects work out they way you hope or believe they will.

(4) Discuss the problems you faced in doing this research project and tell how you tried to overcome them. You might also offer suggestions for carrying out such a study should someone else wish to repeat your research. Frequently social scientists repeat research projects done by other social scientists (a process known as replication) to see whether or not they get the same results.

(5) Attach notes from your interviews to your report. Depth interviews are difficult in the sense that you don't know what you are looking for when you conduct them, and sometimes you don't know what you've found, either. But if we believe that people often act on the bases of attitudes, beliefs, and impulses of which they are unaware, depth interviews have a utility that makes them worth doing.

Aristotle argues that there are three kinds of rhetorical proof; that is, three ways in which a speaker can persuade an audience of his position—ethos, pathos, and logos. *Ethos* is ethical proof, the convincing character of the speaker. . . . *Pathos* is an appeal to the emotions of the audience. . . . *Logos* is logical proof, or argument, the kind of proof that appeals to reason. . . . Our sense of these elements will change according to at least two other primary factors, which are tightly related and which have to do with the nature of the specific discourse. Aristotle's breakdown of the kinds of rhetoric into legislative, judicial, and ceremonial is an acknowledgment that the *aim* of the discourse will determine the form in which it is expressed.

> Robert L. Root, Jr., *The Rhetorics of Popular Culture: Advertising,*
> *Advocacy, and Entertainment* (1987, pp. 16-18)

7

Rhetorical Analysis: Magazine Advertisements

Rhetoric is conventionally defined as the study of persuasion. Aristotle wrote a book, *Rhetoric,* in which he defined rhetoric:

> Rhetoric may be defined as the faculty of observing in any given case the available means of persuasion. This is not the function of any other art. Every other art can instruct or persuade about its own particular subject-matter; for instance, medicine about what is healthy and unhealthy. . . . But rhetoric we look upon as the power of observing the means of persuasion on almost any subject presented to us. (McKeon, 1941, p. 1329)

Rhetoricians typically analyze speech and written language, but the term can also be extended to visual language; we will use this expanded understanding of rhetoric in the research project dealt with in this chapter.

We will investigate how magazine advertisements persuade us to purchase products or services. This means we will try to determine how the copywriters and artists working at advertising agencies use language and images in making magazine advertisements that they believe will "sell."

Problems Faced in Making Rhetorical Analyses

In using rhetorical analysis, we face the question of whether we are applying rhetorical principles correctly. It is one thing to have a list of rhetorical principles (they follow shortly) and another to use them the right way—so as to detect the ways

67

copywriters and artists attempt to convince us to purchase a given product or service.

There is also the matter of which rhetorical principles are best applied to a given advertisement, and whether there are non-rhetorical methods that would be better to use. The answer to this second point is that there are many different techniques that can be used to analyze a text, such as an advertisement (or a film, a television program, a song), and that rhetorical analysis is an important method to use—especially when the matter of persuasion is important.

Advantages of Rhetorical Analysis

Magazine advertisements have been chosen for this exercise in rhetorical analysis because they are easy to obtain and study. Most families subscribe to magazines that are full of advertisements—often there are more pages devoted to advertisements than to editorial copy. Most magazines are targeted toward certain audiences, so we can often gain insights about these audiences by analyzing the advertisements and seeing how the people in the advertising agencies (with lots of studies of these market segments) view them.

Printed advertisements are also easier to deal with than other kinds of advertising—radio or television commercials, for instance. Magazine advertisements contain language and images that stay put and can be studied without having to be transcribed.

Although rhetoric is an ancient and complex subject, an explanation of some of the basic modes of persuasion enables people to make interesting and perceptive analyses. We all are exposed to many printed advertisements during the course of a given day (in newspapers and magazines, on billboards). Quite likely we have thought about some of the printed advertisements we've seen—ones that somehow caught our attention. So this curiosity factor, quite likely, motivates many of us to examine these advertisements more carefully and see how they work.

Disadvantages of Rhetorical Analysis

There is an assumption we make that in analyzing the techniques used in making advertisements persuasive, we obtain insights about the intended audiences of these advertisements. We are, it must be recognized, assuming that people in advertising agencies have correct insights about the targeted segments of the market they are dealing with. Advertisers are not always correct—many advertising campaigns are failures. So we have to be careful when we make generalizations about kinds or types of people and the most effective means that can be used to persuade them.

Another assumption that has often been made is that everyone interprets a particular advertisement (more or less) the same way. We now believe that this is not correct, and that different people, due to such matters as their personalities, education, interests, values, and beliefs, see different things in a given advertisement (or any other *text*—the term that scholars use for works such as commercials, films, television shows, stories, or books). Umberto Eco, an Italian scholar (and novelist) argues that "aberrant decoding" often occurs when we deal with the mass media. This is because of differences between the people who make the advertisements (and encode them in certain and very specific ways) and the audiences (who decode them in a wide variety of ways). Copywriters, for example, may make allusions to a famous work that they assume everyone will know. If people don't know the work, they may not interpret the advertisement correctly.

Rhetorical Analysis Project: A Magazine Advertisement

In this project you will study a magazine advertisement. You will use some of the more common principles of rhetorical analysis to see how images and other visual phenomena (such as type styles) and language in the advertisement have been used to shape a desired response—most typically some kind of "persuasion." This response may be to remember the name of the product, to consider using it or trying it at a later date, or to feel that the product (or service) must be purchased immediately—by calling a toll-free telephone number, for instance.

Rhetorical Devices Used in Persuasion

It is wise to keep in mind an insight provided by Tony Schwartz, in his book *The Responsive Chord* (1974):

> The critical task is to design our package of stimuli so that it resonates with information already stored with the individual and thereby induces the desired learning or behavioral effect. Resonance takes place when the stimuli put into our communication evoke *meaning* in a listener or viewer. That which we put into the communication has no meaning in itself. The meaning of our communication is what a listener or viewer gets *out* of his experience with the communicator's stimulus. (pp. 24-25)

It is much easier to activate impulses and desires in individuals than to convince those individuals starting from scratch. So, in effect, advertisements (we will use the term *advertisement* for print media and *commercial* for radio or television) attempt to "push our buttons." They are stimuli designed to evoke appropriate responses, and we are what might be described as "complicated rats" who participate in the advertisers' experiments.

Metaphoric Language

Metaphoric language communicates through analogy and compares two things. There are two forms of metaphoric language. In a *metaphor*, the analogy is direct: My love *is* a red rose. In a *simile*, the analogy is indirect: My love *is like* a red rose. Sometimes metaphors are found in a sentence's verbs, which suggest the comparison to be made: I *raced*; I *flew*; I *glided*.

Metonymic Language

Metonymic language communicates by association and suggests that something is connected to something else. There are two forms. A *metonym* is a general association: A bowler hat (derby) suggests England. In a *synecdoche,* a part stands for the whole, or vice versa: The White House stands for the American presidency.

We learn to associate many things as we grow up. A few such associations include these:

big houses and wealth
dark shadows and horror
BMWs and yuppies
France and romance
nature and innocence

Clearly this list could be added to almost endlessly. This means that copywriters and art directors in the United States can work with a repertoire of associations that they assume most Americans hold. Advertisements are full of metaphoric and metonymic devices—analogies and associations. If you find any in the advertisement you are studying, you should analyze them and consider how they are used.

Verbal Appeals

In this section a number of the more common appeals and approaches, as reflected in the language, are considered.

Solving a problem. Advertisements often pose a problem (a beautiful woman has no boyfriends because her underarms smell), which they solve (use Zilch underarm deodorant and find the man of your dreams). In some cases, the copywriters create pseudoproblems or magnify trivial ones. They also play upon anxieties people have.

Expert advice. Here the copywriters play upon our desire for reassurance by offering "experts" to give us advice. "More doctors recommend . . . ," they tell us. Sometimes experts are presented who are not really experts in the areas in which they are offering advice.

Comparisons. Here two products are compared, often in a variety of ways, to show that one product is superior to another. You see this in advertisements for cars, computers, and other kinds of complicated machines and devices. Here there is a direct appeal to logic and rationality, but it is sometimes the case that the product's most important aspects are not being considered.

Sexuality

Advertisers use sexuality in a number of different ways for a variety of purposes. One thing they do is play upon our desire for sexual relationships by using attractive women (and, lately, men) and suggestive language in their advertisements. These advertisements play upon our unconscious desires and are designed to arouse us sexually. Women are shown in various stages of undress or using suggestive body language or in scenarios in which sexual activity (in the past or forthcoming) is implied—and this is often reinforced by the language used, which is highly eroticized.

Sometimes, on the other hand, advertisers attempt to create anxieties in our minds about our sexuality and desirability, which they then "solve" by suggesting a product or service for us to use.

Advertisers use sexuality in an attempt to evade rationality (behavior dominated by the ego) and provoke emotional, impulsive acts or decisions (behavior dominated by the id).

Fears and Anxieties

Let me suggest a number of different aspects of this subject. A distinction can be made between anxiety (which is vague and doesn't have a specific object) and fear (which is much more concrete and specific). Generally speaking:

We fear rejection by others.
We fear being lonely.
We fear being unloved.
We fear being different, standing out.

These fears don't apply to everyone, of course, but they tend to apply to most of us. We are social animals and we tend to take comfort in being with others who are like us in one way or another.

Anxieties are much harder to pin down—they are vague, diffuse feelings we sometimes have that plague us. But we can't locate any specific reason for having a given anxiety. We don't generally seem to enjoy being in a state of anxiety and if we can find a way to escape from it, so the logic goes, we will do so.

The Herd Mentality

One way to convince people to buy something is to suggest that "everyone is doing it" and rely on the "herd mentality" in many people, who find safety in numbers. There are, of course, some people who see themselves as individualists and who resist such appeals.

Desire for Approval

Advertisements that take advantage of our desire for the approval of others attempt to convince us that purchasing a particular product or service will merit the approval of those who are members of the "elite" or who are "in the know." Most people want to be approved of by others, and purchasing the right product is posited as a means of obtaining this approval.

Keeping Up with the Joneses

Advertisers often assume that we want to show the world that we are successful and can keep up with others—which means purchasing the kinds of products and doing the kinds of things (taking expensive vacations, sending our kids to the right private schools, driving the right kind of car) that others do. Thorstein Veblen, a famous economic thinker, suggested that "conspicuous display" is a powerful force in human behavior, and keeping up with the Joneses means purchasing products that demonstrate that we are successful.

Imitation of Stars and Celebrities

Although we cannot have the "exciting" and "glamorous" lives that entertainment figures and celebrities have (or tell us they have), we can, at least, use many of the same products they use and that they peddle on television and radio. By doing so, we attain a kind of symbolic identification with them and their life-styles. This "imitation" can also apply to the heroes and heroines they portray in films and television shows.

We identify with celebrities, heroes, and heroines at different stages of our lives and to varying degrees. Advertisers use this process of identification, which can be very powerful, to sell products.

Reward Yourself

Certain advertisers tell us, indirectly and in a subtle manner, to "reward" ourselves by using their products. "You deserve it," they tell us, as payment for your hard work, your diligence, or whatever. The push is for immediate gratification and pleasure without regard for anything else.

Stimulate Fantasy

Perfume advertisements are excellent examples of using fantasy (as well as the desire for sexual gratification) to sell a product. The language tends to be poetic and dreamy and is meant to generate fantasies and daydreams, often of an erotic nature. The product becomes identified with the fantasy. This fantasy is generated by the use of many verbal techniques associated with poetry: alliteration, repetition, rhyme, and highly metaphoric language. This kind of writing is best described as "pseudopoetic," since it is created for commercial purposes.

Slogans and Jingles

Jingles are catchy melodies that are designed to become embedded in our minds. They usually have a strong beat and clever use of language as well and are quite common in radio and television commercials. Slogans are phrases that describe a product or the corporation that manufactures the product. These slogans become identified with the product or corporation—as a kind of verbalized logo. The slogan is repeated over and over in advertisements, often using a particular typeface, to facilitate recognition. Sometimes the slogan is part of a jingle, which further facilitates recognition and memorableness.

A Note on Oppositions

Concepts are based on oppositions; that is why many of the appeals that have been dealt with can be seen as one side of a set of paired opposites. For example:

envy/emulation
anxiety/security
rejection/acceptance
lack/satisfaction
individual/herd mentality
loneliness/popularity

When we look for verbal appeals in magazine advertisements, we should be mindful of the oppositions that are stated or implied in the language.

Images and Visual Phenomena

In this section, we consider images, typefaces, color, and other visual phenomena and the roles they play in "selling" people on products and services.

Balance. As used here, this refers to the physical arrangement of elements in the advertisement. There are two kinds of balance in advertisements: (a) *axial or formal balance*, in which the visual elements are balanced on either side of an imaginary vertical or horizontal line through the center of the advertisement; and (b) *dynamic or informal balance*, in which the visual elements are not arranged in a formal or balanced manner. Generally speaking, we associate formal balance, which has a static quality about it, with sophistication, elegance, and understatement. Most of the time in advertisements we find informal balance, which tends to be more visually exciting.

Spatiality. This refers to the amount of white or empty space in an advertisement. We usually equate white space with sophistication and elite taste. Consider the difference, for example, between a newspaper advertisement for a supermarket, in which this is no white space, and a magazine advertisement for perfume or an expensive watch, which may be full of white space.

Typefaces. Typefaces suggest various things; each face has its own personality. Thin, elegant typefaces generate one feeling and thick, heavy typefaces generate another. There are hundreds of different typefaces and many sizes of each face. In thinking about the typefaces used, consider the product, its potential market, the life-style and taste of people in this market, and the appropriateness of the typefaces used. Remember that there is a conscious decision, usually by a typographer, behind the choice of every typeface and decisions about the size of the typeface and the amount of space between lines of type.

Color. What colors are used in the advertisement and what significance do they have? Is the coloration bright or subdued? What might that mean? Does the coloration suggest sophistication and restraint, or passion and raw energy? Is color being used to be realistic or to stylize the product in some way?

Camera shots and angles. If there is a photographic image in the advertisement, what kind of camera shot is involved? If there are a number of photographic images, what are they like and why were they chosen? Do we look down on some scenario or do we look up at one? Is the shot a close-up or an extreme long shot? Are we level with the action? Why was the particular camera shot and angle chosen?

Models. There are a number of things to consider concerning the appearance of human beings, animals, and other models in advertisements:

- *gender:* male or female
- *age:* young, old, middle-aged
- *facial characteristics:* regularity of features, color of hair, eyes, complexion of skin, and the like
- *facial expressions:* emotions shown
- *body language:* attitudes shown by posture, position of limbs, and the like
- *life-style props:* hairstyles, clothes worn, eyeglass styles, and so on
- *relationships implied:* by scenario, language in copy

Carrying Out a Rhetorical Analysis
of a Magazine Advertisement

(1) You should select a magazine advertisement that has an image and a substantial amount of printed matter (copy). It is hard to analyze persuasive techniques used in an advertisement that has only a few words of copy.

(2) You should also select an advertisement that is visually interesting, so you can deal with the ways images and other visual materials are used to support the verbal material.

(3) Use the list of rhetorical (persuasive) devices discussed above to analyze your text.

Writing Up Your Rhetorical Analysis

(1) Write an introduction in which you give the reader a general overview of what you are doing—making a rhetorical analysis of a magazine advertisement in terms of the language and visual elements found in it. It would be useful to say something about the nature of rhetorical analysis and the way you are using it. Attach the advertisement to your paper, so the reader can see what you are discussing.

(2) Tell the reader what interesting things you found in the advertisement, referring to such things as the copy (language) and visual elements. You probably will want to discuss specific aspects of the language and the visual devices used. Make sure you support your contentions with evidence that a reasonable person might find persuasive. That is, you should have some reasons or justifications for the points you make. In the case of your analysis of the language, for example, you should tie some rhetorical concept to your point.

If you consulted any books on rhetorical analysis or on advertising, you can make use of any information you found in these works by relating it to your analysis. Even though you might not have found an analysis of the particular advertisements you were investigating, you can discuss information about advertising, images, and other related concerns that applies to your research.

(3) Discuss any interesting insights or conclusions that stem from your research. Did your research help you discover something you consider important? Did you obtain any insights from the research?

(4) Discuss any important problems you encountered in doing this research and any qualifications you wish to make about your findings or any generalizations you made based on your findings. (Remember, it is a good idea to qualify generalizations and to avoid making extreme *all* or *every* statements.)

An important part of the preparation for research work consists in learning how to use the resources of libraries. It is important because all research inevitably involves the use of the book, pamphlet, periodical, and documentary materials in libraries. This applies to studies based on original data gathered in a field study as well as those based entirely upon documentary sources. In both types of studies there is the same need for using certain basic kinds of published materials. On the one hand, general source materials have to be consulted for the necessary background knowledge of the problem to be investigated. Obviously, no research project can be undertaken without this preliminary orientation. Nor should one be undertaken without knowledge of the research that has already been done in the field. It provides further orientation to the problem, and at the same time eliminates the possibility of unnecessary duplication of effort. In addition, valuable information on research techniques may be gained from reports of previous research.

Joseph S. Komidar, "The Uses of the Library," in William J. Goode and Paul K. Hatt, *Methods in Social Research* (1952, p. 103)

8

Library Research:
Audiences of Radio Talk Shows

Searching in a library for information on a particular subject can
be very much like looking for a needle in a haystack, especially
if you don't know how to conduct your search. One of the more
important topics librarians concern themselves with nowadays
is "information retrieval," or, in everyday language, finding
what one is looking for in a library. Many major university
libraries have millions of books in them, plus magazines, newspapers, and all kinds of other documents (often in many different languages, as well), and new material is coming in all the
time. Thousands of new books are published every year in the
United States, as well as seemingly countless numbers of scholarly journals, popular magazines, and government reports.

Librarians often face formidable problems in determining
where to put what. For example, suppose a book is published
that is a history of political philosophy. Does the book go in the
history section, the political science section, or the philosophy
section of the library? Fortunately, this is a problem that cata-
loguers have to face, not us. What is important for us is to be
able to find the book (or whatever information we want) when
we need it.

The purpose of the library search, as far as we are concerned, is to obtain relevant information, by experts and reliable sources, that helps answer some question. When students
write typical term papers, they try to find quotations from experts and authorities (relevant sources) that help them deal with
some question or issue. The students gather material, which

they then assemble into an argument, using the quotations from
their experts to support their positions and the conclusions they
reach from their research.

You do research because you want to know something. In
some cases, you can never find an answer that everyone will
accept. For example, suppose you want to prove that the San
Francisco 49ers are the greatest football team of all time. You
can assemble data, statistics, and so on, but this is a topic that
can never be resolved, because there are no generally accepted
criteria for proving something like this. There are other questions of a similar nature: Was Napoleon "good" or "bad"? What
"caused" the Civil War? The important point here is that some
questions can never be answered in a way that will satisfy
everyone, so you must be careful about the questions you ask
and what problems you select for your research. "Why" questions and evaluative questions are difficult to deal with.

It is possible that for an assignment you will need to get
information on some recent historical event. You can find, in the
library, reports from eyewitnesses (in the form of newspaper
articles, books, diaries, journals, radio and television programs,
and so on) and articles and books by scholars (who, we presume, have conducted a variety of different kinds of research).
The material you gather is then used as "evidence" in your
paper. You may use this material in the form of either paraphrases or direct quotations. In all cases, you must acknowl-
edge where you got your information.

You use your evidence the way a prosecuting attorney uses
witnesses in an attempt to convict a person who is accused of
some crime. And, as in a trial, there may be conflicting reports
by witnesses about what "really" happened. What do you do
when "experts" and "authorities" disagree with one another—
which is often the case? You have to decide which expert or
authority is most credible, and why.

Sometimes just digging out facts is quite a problem, and you
may have assignments that ask nothing more of you than getting information about some topic. But generally you will be
asked to do more than find facts; you will be asked to assemble
information that will support some kind of a thesis, some kind
of a generalization.

Problems in Doing Library Research

You may find it difficult to locate relevant sources. What do you do if you can't find anything on the subject? How do you start searching for information on the subject? In looking for information, you might want to consult some of the following sources:

- the library's card catalogue (often on computer now)
- data bases on various topics, often found in libraries
- encyclopedias and reference works of various kinds
- indexes to periodicals, such as the *Reader's Guide*, the *New York Times Index*, and *Book Review Digest*
- bibliographies devoted to specific topics
- textbooks and scholarly journals, which often have substantial bibliographies
- research librarians
- the popular media—newspapers, magazines, best-sellers, videos of news shows and television programs, and the like

You must get up-to-date information. You should try to get the most recent work on whatever topic it is you are researching. If all of your sources are 10 or 15 years old (in some cases, even a couple of years old), you will be downgraded for using "dated" material. Suppose you are doing a project on the Civil War. You would be perfectly correct to use material written by people who were in the war (diaries) and by people who observed it (newspaper reporters, historians of the time, and politicians) but you would also want to have the latest interpretations of modern-day historians, which you might find in scholarly journals.

Historians, remember, disagree on many things, because historians interpret what went on in the past. They don't tell you what happened, but rather what they think happened. That applies to scholars in other disciplines as well.

Advantages of Library Searches

Library searches don't cost anything if you do them yourself. If you use a computer and do a search using some data base, there may be a charge for the service—sometimes such costs are considerable. But if you use your own resources and confine yourself to material in the card catalogue of the library you are using, research costs nothing.

In doing library research you don't have the difficult problems that often come from "designing research" and you don't have to deal with people (as in a depth interview, survey, or experiment). You don't have to worry about whether or not people will cooperate with you and be truthful. Your basic problem is finding information that you presume is in the library but in locations that you don't know.

Disadvantages of Library Searches

One fundamental problem with this kind of research is that the material you get is usually something that has been filtered through someone else's mind—that of some writer or photographer or editor. You are always dealing, in a sense, with secondhand information.

Sometimes libraries don't have the books and periodicals you need, or they have them and you can locate them but when you go to get them you discover that they have been checked out or are misfiled or lost (or stolen).

Despite these difficulties, libraries (especially at universities) are remarkable institutions, and it is amazing how much material they have. Students aren't the only people who do library research. Many people in the media and in various other professions use libraries to get the information they need.

For the project you are asked to do for this chapter, on talk shows, you will need a university library—one that has scholarly journals that deal with broadcasting, communications, popular culture, journalism, and the mass media. Public libraries—city and county libraries—often have many popular periodicals that have material on these subjects, but it is usually not material written by scholars, which is necessary for this exercise.

Library Search Assignment:
Audiences of Radio Talk Shows

(1) In this exercise, find the latest material on audiences of radio talk shows and on related topics such as the following:

- who listens to radio talk shows and, of related interest, any changes over the years in the demographics of audiences of radio talk shows
- the effects of these talk shows on people and on society
- why people listen (or say they listen) to radio talk shows

Obtain this material by finding research journals that deal with the mass media and related areas. We use research journals because generally they are more up to date than books. It takes more than a year to publish a book, while journals often appear quarterly, so it is in journals that we generally find reports of the newest research.

(2) Try to find as many scholarly sources as you can. You should also consult books that may have material on radio talk shows, to see whether the journal articles support what is in the books or have new findings that contradict or modify them in some way.

There is a great deal of research done on radio talk shows, but most of it is proprietary; that is, it is paid for by radio stations that will not, generally, share the findings with others. You may, however, be able to obtain some data about the popularity of various talk shows from public relations departments of radio stations and in broadcasting trade journals and reports by ratings organizations.

Some newspapers carry columns on radio that may be of use, but your main sources should be research articles by scholars. You might find the material you are looking for in some of the following sources:

- books on the subject
- chapters on the subject within more general books
- scholarly articles in scholarly journals

- popular articles in magazines read by the general public; also articles in trade journals
- newspaper articles
- encyclopedia articles such as those found in the *Encyclopedia of Communication*, published by the Oxford University Press
- abstracts of scholarly articles

In doing this research, you are working within a very large field called *communications*. You can narrow your search for information by considering the following:

- Communications is your general area.
- The mass media make up a subcategory of this area.
- Electronic media make up a subcategory of mass media.
- Broadcast media make up a subcategory of electronic media.
- Radio is a subcategory of electronic media.
- Talk shows are a genre or kind of program carried on radio.
- The audiences of talk shows make up a subject related to talk shows.

You may find material that is relevant in any area of this list of categories and subcategories. For example, some theories of communications may help explain why audiences of radio talk shows behave the way they do, so there are many different areas that can be investigated in looking for useful information on radio talk shows. Don't assume that you can use only articles on audiences of radio talk shows—though you certainly should have some research articles on them as well as data about them.

Writing Up Your Research Project

(1) Write an introduction in which you give the reader an idea of the general background of your subject, an overview, a sense of context. You might give a brief history of the development of radio talk shows and say something about their importance before discussing the questions you investigated in doing your research.

(2) Tell the reader what your research questions were and what your conclusions are. You should explain how you went about getting information, what you found, and how you arrived at your conclusions. If you found articles that differed

---

Exhibit 8.1
How to Read Analytically

(1) *Look for important concepts and ideas* and how they are explained and used. Is the concept "materialism" used? If so, how is it defined and employed by the writer?

(2) *Look for factual material, data, and statistics* that are used to support arguments.

(3) *Look for arguments made by the author.* Why does the author believe or not believe something? What methodologies are employed?

(4) *Look for contrasts and comparisons.* Frequently authors embed these in their texts. When you can, make a chart that shows these contrasts and comparisons.

(5) *Look at the examples used.* Are they relevant? Do they support assertions? Or are they too selective, neglecting other examples that might not support these assertions?

(6) *Look for threads*, topics that keep coming up repeatedly. What significance do these threads have?

(7) *Look for insights*—this can be understood as seeing relationships between or among phenomena that you never saw before. Are these insights valuable? Where do they lead you?

(8) *Don't expect to agree with everything an author writes.* If you disagree, make sure you have valid reasons. Even if authors are wrong about some things, they may be right about other things.

(9) *Consider adaptations you can make.* For example, essays on the nature of heroes and heroines in Greek mythology can sometimes be applied to characters in the mass media in interesting ways. You may not be able to find an article on a particular situation comedy, but you may find material on situation comedies in general or on humor that you can apply.

(10) *What about the author's style?* How important is style in convincing you to believe something? What is distinctive about the author's style?

(11) *What sources does the author quote from?* Do these sources give you any ideas about the author's point of view, politics, values, seriousness?

NOTE: You should keep these considerations in mind when you write, for readers will be using these analytical notions to interpret your papers.

---

with one another on topics such as how many people listen to these shows, who listens, why they listen, and the effects of these shows on listeners and society in general, explain how you evaluated the conflicting material and why you came to the conclusions you did.

(3) Provide the reader with data and other reasons to accept your conclusions. If you have to qualify your conclusions, explain why. If you had any difficulties in doing your research, explain what they were and how you dealt with them. In addition to discussing the problems you faced, offer suggestions for any researcher who may wish to undertake similar research.

(4) Provide some kind of wrap-up at the end of your paper, so you reader isn't left hanging. There are several methods you can use. One is to summarize what you have found, so the reader gets a good general view of what you have done. The other is to discuss implications of your work and, perhaps, a refinement of the earlier conclusion that emerged from your paper. Whatever the case, don't leave the reader hanging by stopping abruptly because, perhaps, you have reached the minimum number of pages required in your assignment.

If you were out in the so-called real world and had a job as a reporter for a newspaper or television station, you would employ the same techniques you will be using in carrying out this assignment. We live in an information age, as I've said before, and most people who work in the information society constantly find themselves searching for information on a wide variety of subjects.

Let me conclude by quoting the first paragraph of the first chapter of an excellent book, *Search Strategies in Mass Communication*, by Jean Ward and Kathleen A. Hansen (1987):

> The news assignment: an article or series of articles on gentrification, or the displacement of urban poor from old neighborhoods that are undergoing rehabilitation. The reporter: a generalist who must begin by recognizing her own lack of knowledge about this subject. The challenge: to do a rapid study of gentrification. The sources: knowledgeable people and reputable books and articles. In conducting her survey of what is known about the subject, the well-prepared reporter will range widely and consult experts in such fields as economics, architecture, insurance, banking, housing, city planning, demographics, race relations, urban affairs, and tax policy. Her choice of people to be

interviewed will be influenced by what she learns in her overview of the subject. Her questions to interviewers will be shaped partly by a need to expand on and to update what she learns in her first study of the subject. (p. 1)

You will not be asked to interview people in this exercise, but you will be doing the same kind of thing the mythical reporter described above was asked to do.

Library searches are not make-work, designed by malicious professors interested only in making your life miserable. The library search is a tool that you can use and will use in your career, for one of the most important things students can learn is how to continue learning, how to find information on subjects that interest them. There is now so much information available that nobody can keep up with it. What is important is being able to find information when you want it.

In late August and early September, with the story of John Zaccaro's finances dominating the news, the wounded Democratic campaign tested image and issues ads to use in the race against Reagan. The findings of focus groups conducted by Edward J. Reilly of Boston say a great deal about the problems Mondale faced and offer feedback concerning how a presidential campaign can evaluate its advertising effort. The lessons might equally apply to any candidate attempting to develop a coherent message after his or her credibility has been severely damaged.

In a series of "Mondale to Camera" ads tested on September 4, the Reilly group concluded that respondents were "distracted by the visuals and by his presence" and "had difficulty understanding the message" concerning education, taxes, and the deficit. Several remarked that Mondale might be right on the issues, but they didn't "see how he's going to do it." One undecided farmer reached the conclusion most feared by the Mondale campaign: "He reminds me of Carter in those ads."

Montague Kern, *30-Second Politics:*
Political Advertising in the Eighties (1989, pp. 118-119)

9

Focus Groups:
Reasons for Attending Films

Focus groups are group interviews that are held to find out how people feel about some product, service, or issue. A group of people are assembled and a free-form discussion is held, led by a moderator, to obtain the desired information. As Roger D. Wimmer and Joseph R. Dominick write in *Mass Media Research: An Introduction* (1983), "The focus group technique involves interviewing two or more people simultaneously, with a moderator or facilitator leading the respondents in a relatively free discussion about the topic under consideration" (p. 100). The subject is usually the attitudes and behavior of the people in the group relative to some consumer product or choice (as in elections) they might wish to make.

The aim of the discussion is not to build consensus, but just the opposite—to find out what each member of the focus group thinks about the topic under discussion, to elicit from each person in the group his or her opinions and descriptions of behavior of interest. Focus groups are, then, probes that are meant to find out how people think and act. They are a kind of collective depth interview, and it is hoped that the discussion will lead to important insights that will help manufacturers of products or sellers of services function more efficiently.

Problems with Focus Groups

The first problem involves getting a representative group of people together to form the focus group. If you want to find out about how people respond to a new product that is being developed to compete with an established product, you must find people who use the product, or who might be persuaded to use it. In actuality, it is not too difficult to assemble focus groups. There are companies that have a good deal of expertise in assembling these groups and in running focus group interviews. Participants are often paid a small sum to be part of focus groups and often find it rather pleasant, being with a group of people chatting about some topic and having their opinions count for something.

In this research technique, the ability of the moderator is crucial. Moderators must not be directive or too assertive, but they must also make sure the discussion doesn't get off track. As Jean Ward and Kathleen A. Hansen write in *Search Strategies in Mass Communication* (1987):

> The moderator of a focus group lets the discussion range while it is moving productively and producing useful comment. Tasks include making certain that main points are covered, being receptive to new points that arise, and making sure that each respondent has a chance to talk. (p. 178)

Leading discussions is often difficult. It takes a light touch and a good deal of skill to get everyone to contribute.

Advantages of Focus Group Research

Focus groups are a relatively inexpensive way to do research. The moderator must be paid and members are generally given a small payment for participating, but this is still a great deal less expensive than making a survey. According to Wimmer and Dominick (1983), the price range can be from as little as a few hundred dollars to as expensive as several thousand dollars "depending on the size of the group, the difficulties in sample selection, and the company that conducts the group" (p. 101). Focus groups are often used in advertising and market research and several thousand dollars is a relatively small percentage of the money that is spent in research and the production of advertising.

Focus groups can be assembled quickly, and the insights of the people in the focus groups are immediately available. Focus groups are often audiotaped and can be easily videotaped so that, in addition to their opinions, respondents' body language and other aspects of their behavior can be analyzed in some detail. Audiotaping and videotaping can be done unobtrusively.

Focus groups also provide a great degree of interviewing flexibility. The moderator can easily follow up on some response a member of the group makes, can ask questions, solicit opinions, raise issues, and so on. He or she can follow chance leads and obtain valuable information firsthand.

Group dynamics work so that respondents often become caught up in the discussion and stimulate other members to contribute, sometimes offering information that is very useful. In a group situation, inhibitions and the like can often be overcome, and material buried in the psyche can be accessed.

Disadvantages of Focus Group Research

Because of the nature of focus groups there is a problem with the generalizability of results. A focus group represents a relatively small group of people, and they may not be representative of the potential users of a product or service. That is why it is important to assemble focus groups carefully.

The data from focus groups does not lend itself to quantification. One gets opinions, attitudes, recollections of past behavior (which may be incorrect), and that kind of thing. One gets answers to "why" questions, not "how many" questions, which is why some researchers think focus groups are primarily useful for making pilot studies or as a complement to other kinds of studies.

Some participants in focus groups tend to monopolize the conversation and must be restrained without inhibiting other members of the group. Conversely, some members of the group might be shy and have to be drawn out without being made uncomfortable.

Members of the focus group may be inhibited by being tape-recorded (and video-recorded, if that is done). They must be told by the moderator that they are being audiotaped or video-taped; it would be extremely unethical to record people without their knowing it. Members of these groups have to sign releases, and this may inhibit some people.

Focus Group Project:
How People Decide Which Films to Attend

In this project you will try to find out why people go to some films and not others—that is, what is most important in their decision making. You will limit your group to students and, to make things easier, take some already-assembled group of stu-dents (such as a group of three or four people having lunch at the school cafeteria) to function as your ad hoc focus group. Members of some club or other entity who would be willing to spend some time (perhaps a half hour) can also be used.

Generally speaking, the moderator of a focus group has a list of questions to be dealt with. In the case of film choice, the following possibilities suggest themselves. The most important reason people go to a particular film might be one of the following:

(1) the director
(2) the stars
(3) the genre
(4) word of mouth
(5) reviews
(6) cheapest theater
(7) nearest theater
(8) went with friends who made choice

The function of the discussion is *not* to get members of the group to agree on one or more reasons, but to find out how or why each member decides to go to a film. We are concerned about past behavior—why respondents have acted the way they did. But opinions of respondents about why they think people decide to go to one film rather than another are also useful.

Suggestions for Moderators

Here are the procedures you should follow once you have found the group of people who will be functioning as your focus group.

(1) Explain the purpose of the focus group—how focus groups work, what their function is, and so on. If possible, taperecord the discussion. Explain that you are recording the discussion so you can quote people accurately in the report you will be writing. If you don't have a tape recorder or access to one, take careful notes and do the best you can.

(2) Make the members of the group feel at ease. Explain to them that nobody is wrong in focus groups, that all opinions are valuable.

(3) Get any demographic information that might be useful or interesting.

(4) Don't direct the discussion, but draw people out, to the extent that you can. Focus groups are nondirective.

(5) Follow up on "leads" you get. That is, if someone says something that you think is interesting and has important implications, draw him or her out on the matter. And ask others for their comments.

(6) Try to get everyone involved in the discussion; don't allow anyone to dominate or monopolize things.

(7) Make sure you stick to the subject and don't go off on tangents. For instance, respondents might want to discuss the films they have just seen instead of why they chose to see these films; you must guard against the discussion going off track.

(8) Repeat back to people occasionally what you understand them to have said, as a means of clarifying things and perhaps stimulating others to contribute to the discussion.

(9) At certain times, ask specific members of the focus group for their opinions, instead of making generalized requests ("Does anyone have an opinion on this?").

Writing a Report on
Your Focus Group Discussion

(1) Offer a brief introduction in which you describe the makeup of your focus group and discuss the topic you researched.

(2) List and discuss, in order of importance, the reasons your respondents gave as being most important in their decisions about what movies to attend. Offer significant quotations and explain their importance.

(3) Did you have any preliminary hypotheses in mind before you led the focus group? What led you to these hypotheses? How do you feel about your hypotheses after leading the focus group?

(4) What (if any) insights, revelations, or unusual findings did you make as a result of conducting the focus group? What conclusions did you come to? Remember to qualify your generalizations, especially if your focus group was small and ad hoc (fashioned from what was immediately available).

(5) Did you experience any difficulties in carrying out this project? If so, describe them.

PART II

Writing and Thinking

Metaphor is pervasive in everyday life, not just in language but in thought and action. Our ordinary conceptual system, in terms of which we both think and act, is fundamentally metaphorical in nature.

The concepts that govern our thought are not just matters of the intellect. They also govern our everyday functioning, down to the most mundane details. Our concepts structure what we perceive, how we get around in the world, and how we relate to other people. Our conceptual system thus plays a central role in defining our everyday realities. If we are right in suggesting that our conceptual system is largely metaphorical, then the way we think, what we experience, and what we do every day is very much a matter of metaphor.

George Lakoff and Mark Johnson, *Metaphors We Live By* (1980, p. 3)

10

Writing with Style

Rhetoric, as was discussed in Chapter 7, is technically defined as the "science of persuasion." For our purposes here, however, we will consider rhetoric to deal with effective writing. This chapter discusses a number of techniques that can be used in writing so that readers will find it interesting, entertaining, informative, fascinating, and easy to understand.

It is not a bad idea (even if it isn't true) to assume that all readers are reluctant and would rather be watching television. In order to get people to read something you have written, then, you must take pains to attract their attention, gain their interest, and make it easy (and desirable) for them to continue reading what you have written. You must cater to certain needs people have—curiosity about what causes things, what effects things have, how something differs from something else, and so on.

A number of rhetorical techniques are discussed below. Many of these techniques are signaled in writing by the use of transitions. The following chart, adapted from my book *Scripts: Writing for Radio and Television* (1990), shows some of the more important transitions and their functions:

Offering Examples	Conclusions Reached	Argument Continues
for example	therefore	furthermore
for instance	thus	in addition
as an illustration	we find, then	to continue
to show this	to sum up	similarly
Contrasting Ideas	*Causes*	*Effects*
but	because	as a result
however	since	therefore
on the other hand	this leads to	accordingly
in contrast	seeing that	as a consequence

Sequence	Time Relation	Meaning
first	before	this means
next	after	we find, then
furthermore	meanwhile	this suggests
to begin with	at the same time	this tells us

For more on transitional elements, see Exhibit 10.1. We will now consider some of the more important ways you can make your writing more interesting and appealing.

Contrast and Comparison

Contrast and comparison are important because, as was pointed out earlier, we find meaning in things by comparing them (and contrasting them) with other things. *Rich* doesn't mean anything unless there is *poor*; *intelligent* doesn't mean anything unless there is *dumb*. Meaning stems from differentiations we make, and the most significant differentiations we make involve oppositions. We know that there are rich people, middle-class people, and poor people (and many gradations in between, as well), but we commonly think of opposites when making comparisons.

Items or concepts that are contrasted and compared must have something in common, a category that can be applied to all of them. We generally indicate that we are making a contrast by using a transition such as "on the other hand" or "for a contrasting view." We do the same for comparisons, using transitions such as "in the same manner."

Definitions

Definitions are statements recording how people use words. That is, a definition tells us how people use (or used) a term, the conventions common in using the term, or what people "mean" by a term. Thus a dictionary is a record that shows how people use words; in some cases, dictionaries also show the roots (in Latin, Greek, and other languages) of words.

It is often the case that researchers define words in certain ways for the purposes of their work. The word *violence* is a good

---

Exhibit 10.1
Transitional Elements

Here is an example of writing in which transitional elements are used; all bold type has been added to emphasize the transitions. I have selected this passage because it shows how transitions order thinking and because it contains advice of considerable importance and usefulness for writers.

How Judgments Stop Thought

A judgment ("He is a fine boy," "It was a beautiful service," "Baseball is a healthful sport," "She is an awful bore") is a conclusion, summing up a large number of previously observed facts. The reader is probably familiar with the fact that students almost always have difficulty in writing themes of the required length because their ideas give out after a paragraph or two. **The reason for this is that** those early paragraphs contain so many judgments that there is little left to be said. When the conclusions are carefully excluded, **however,** and observed facts are given instead, there is never any trouble about the length of papers; **in fact,** they tend to become too long, **since** inexperienced writers, when told to give facts, often give far more than is necessary, **because** they lack discrimination between the important and the trivial.

Still another consequence of judgments early in the course of a written exercise—and this applies also to hasty judgments in everyday thought—is the temporary blindness they induce. When, **for example,** a description starts with the words, "He was a real Madison Avenue executive" or "She was a typical hippie," if we continue writing at all, we must make all our later statements consistent with those judgments. **The result is** that all the individual characteristics of this particular "executive" or this particular "hippie" are lost sight of; **and** the rest of the account is likely to deal not with observed facts but with stereotypes and the writer's particular notion (based on previously read stories, movies, pictures, and so forth) of what "Madison Avenue executives" or "typical hippies" are like. The premature judgment, **that is,** often prevents us from seeing what is directly in front of us, **so that** clichés take the place of fresh description. **Therefore,** even if the writer feels sure at the beginning of a written account that the man he is describing is a "real leatherneck" or that the scene he is describing is a "beautiful residential suburb," he will conscientiously keep such notions out of his head, lest his vision be obstructed. He is specifically warned against describing anybody as a "beatnik"—a term (originally applied to literary and artistic Bohemians) which was blown up by sensational journalism and movies into an almost completely fictional and misleading stereotype. If a writer applies the term to any actual living human being, he will have to expend so much energy thereafter explaining what he does *not* mean by it that he will save himself trouble by not bringing it up at all. The same warning applies to "hippies" and other social classifications that tend to submerge the individual in a category.

SOURCE: Hayakawa (1978, p. 40).

example. The amount of violence a researcher finds on television is affected by the way he or she defines the term. Researchers who use a very narrow definition of *violence* will, logically, find less violence on television than those who use a very broad, all-encompassing definition of the term (and include, for instance, humorous violence and accidental violence). Because there are so many different aspects of violence, it is a good idea for researchers in this field to explain how they are using the term and to offer reasonable explanations for their definition.

In some cases, it is useful to cite an expert or authority when offering a definition. Let me offer an example. It has been estimated that there are more than 100 definitions by anthropologists of the term *culture*—and there are countless other definitions by literary scholars and other kinds of academics. If you are dealing with culture from an anthropological perspective (and we are doing that in this book), it is a good idea to explain what you mean by the term. The following definition is from Henry Pratt Fairchild's *Dictionary of Sociology and Related Sciences (Your College Course at a Glance)* (1967):

> A collective name for all behavior patterns socially acquired and transmitted by means of symbols; hence a name for all the distinctive achievements of human groups, including not only such items as language, tool-making, industry, art, science, law, government, morals and religion, but also the material instruments or artifacts in which cultural achievements are embodied and by which intellectual cultural features are given practical effect, such as buildings, tools, machines, communications devices, art objects, etc. (p. 80)

According to this definition everybody has culture; indeed, to be human is to become, in the anthropological sense of the term, cultured. This definition gives us a considerably different perspective on things from one that equates culture with the "elite" arts such as opera, classical music, ballet, serious novels, and poetry.

It is generally a good idea to define terms that may be unfamiliar to your readers or that you are using in a special way.

Cause and Effect

Cause and effect form probably the most common "explanation" we use. When we explain something we usually try to explain what it was that brought the situation about. What "caused" the Civil War? What are the "causes" of poverty?

One of the reasons we are interested in causes is that we believe we can gain some measure of control over things once we have determined what causes them. If you have an upset stomach, it is helpful to know what is causing it—so you can take the right kind of medicine, and, also, so you can avoiding eating foods that you have trouble digesting. Or maybe it wasn't the kind of food you ate but where you ate it. Perhaps you had dinner in a restaurant that wasn't as clean as it should be?

Thus we search for causes to help us understand and explain effects, so we can prevent effects we don't want and generate effects we do want. The basic dimension we deal with is time. The cause, naturally, comes before the effect—but just because Y occurred after X doesn't mean Y was caused by X. Assuming that something is a cause because it precedes an effect is known as the *post hoc, ergo propter hoc* (after, therefore as a result of) fallacy. Consider, for example, an upset stomach. There can be any number of reasons a person might have an upset stomach: food poisoning, too much food, too much exercise after eating, being allergic to certain kinds of food, and so on. When dealing with cause and effect, then, it is generally a good idea to qualify statements and say that there is reason to believe that something "seems to" cause or "might be" causing a given effect.

Classification

The purpose of classification is to find relationships that are not immediately evident. Classification involves taking some collection or group of people or objects or events that have something in common and showing what they share. That is, we take a group related by some common attribute or attributes and break the group down further into mutually exclusive subgroups—depending upon what we want to find out.

For example, take a group of students in one of your classes. What they have in common that makes them a "class" is that they are in the same room with the same teacher taking the same course at the same time. This same group can be broken down into smaller groups in terms of such characteristics as socio-economic class, race, religion, gender, major, hair color, and marital status. By classifying groups we often find interesting information. Some groups may be underrepresented, other groups overrepresented. You may discover that class members are similar in a number of different ways, and that may be important. There are any number of ways of classifying any "class"—depending upon the purpose being served.

Sometimes, instead of breaking a group of persons or things into subclasses related in some way, you will do the opposite and set up a classification system for some grouping or seemingly disparate people or events. In this case, you look for relationships among them and set up a classification scheme that shows how they are related.

Marketing researchers are always coming up with new classification schemes that divide the American public into various groupings. One recent example, called VALS, deals with values and life-styles among Americans and suggests that there are three main categories: the need-driven, the outer-directed, and the inner-directed. There are a number of subcategories under each of these main categories:

need-driven	outer-directed	inner-directed
survivors	belongers	I-am-me
sustainers	emulators	experiential
achievers	societally conscious	

The idea behind VALS is that if we understand what the people in each of these groupings and subgroupings are like, we can direct advertising to them in a more intelligent and effective manner. Different appeals would be used to sell products to emulators (who imitate others) than to achievers (who tend to be individualists), for instance.

Analysis

Analysis is similar to classification, except that instead of dealing with a collection of items, analysis deals with one item or entity. Classification means breaking down a group into subgroups and showing how they are related. Analysis means separating something into its component parts or elements in order to see relationships better and to gain information.

Consider, for example, the drug crisis stemming from "crack" cocaine. An analysis of this crisis might consider such matters as the following: the production of crack; the distribution of crack; various kinds of other drugs available; the reasons some people use crack and others don't; the impact of crack on individuals, families (especially babies born suffering crack addition), and society; ways of preventing crack use and other drug abuse; and new drugs that might compete with or displace crack (such as "ice"). We analyze something such as the crack crisis to see what the component parts are and to get a better sense of how to deal with it. Our analysis may suggest that a certain course of action is most likely to help us achieve the results we want. We analyze, then, to understand.

Examples

The use of examples is one of the best ways to make yourself clear. Explanations, of almost anything, tend to be rather abstract—because they generally have to cover a wide variety of possibilities. When you move down the ladder of abstraction from explanation to examples, however, you provide a means for your reader to see more clearly what you are talking about.

Examples are a kind of evidence that help document a generalization. An example is a "case history" that is both specific and has implications beyond itself. You must be sure that your example is relevant to the point you are making.

There are a number of transitional devices (as shown above) that help "cue" your reader than an example will follow. When you write "for example," your reader knows you are now going to offer something specific.

For example, talking about "juvenile delinquency" is rather abstract. It is useful to move to a case study of a young person who broke six windows in a school, set fire to the school, stole a car, robbed a gas station, mugged an old lady, and so on to show your readers what you mean by the term *juvenile delinquent*. It is always a good idea to *show* people what you are talking about, and you do this by using examples. It is also useful to move back and forth between generalizations and abstractions and examples. If you write at too high a level of abstraction, your writing lacks interest; if you deal only with examples, you can't make any interesting generalizations.

Description and Detail

Description is another important way of developing your writing style and providing your readers with material they will find interesting and illuminating. Many people do not have what might be described as a "developed" style of writing. Their writing has no flesh attached to the bare bones of their prose; there is no description of anything, no detail.

To see the difference description and detail make, think of a meal as it might be described by two different people. The first person writes, "We had a delicious meal at Pierre's last night." This is undeveloped writing—it offers little information and tells you something but provides nothing to support the generalization "delicious." The second writer, a restaurant critic, describes in great detail each and every dish, how it was made, how it was served, what it tasted like, what it looked like, and so on. The second writer might have written:

> We began with a dish of escargot—six plump escargot, swimming in a smooth and exquisitely subtle sauce of butter, garlic, and parsley. The escargot were served on a piping hot china dish. . . .

The description of the meal might take pages, with whole paragraphs devoted to a particular dish, its sauces, its taste, and related matters.

When students complain that they don't have enough material to write a paper of five or ten pages, it is generally because the students don't write in a developed style and don't offer enough description and detail. The other side of the matter, of course, is that you must not use description and detail in an inappropriate manner—simply to pad your papers. You have to use some judgment in deciding when to use description and detail, examples, or any of the other rhetorical techniques discussed here.

Process

Process deals with how something works, how something is to be done, what must be done to accomplish something. This might be something as simple as baking a cake or as complicated as discussing how a research project was carried out. In a sense, process is a kind of description, except that the focus in process is on the way something works or has been done, while description tends to be more static, and tells what something is like.

In writing up your findings, it is important for you to deal with process and describe what you did when you conducted your research. This will enable those who read your write-up to follow the way you worked and see whether or not you made any mistakes. Writing about process is sequential—you describe the various steps you took, one after another, in carrying out your research. This covers everything from the assignment of the research method to the writing up of the conclusions.

Tone

Tone has to do with the degree of formality used in writing. You determine the proper tone to adopt by considering your audience. If you are writing a letter to a friend, your tone will be much more informal, casual, and conversational than it would be if you were writing a letter to apply for a job or if you were writing a paper for a course.

You should always take the matter of formality or informality into consideration and adopt the appropriate tone. Generally speaking, papers written for courses in schools and universities

are written in a formal style, unless you have been given in-
structions to the contrary. You should avoid a casual, conversational tone in research papers, but this does not mean your
writing has to be stilted or affected.

Often, first-person plurals or third person is used in writing
formal papers (although this style is no longer absolutely required). We write "we" or use phrases such as "the author" or
"the investigator" when we want to mention ourselves. Or we
avoid mentioning ourselves and just write about what we did.
The main thing about formal writing is not so much the tone,
however, as the need to support contentions with evidence and
to avoid grammatical and logical errors. Adopting an elevated
or stilted style and using jargon are not substitutes for good
thinking and good writing.

Structure

Structure means the organization of the paper—the relationship that is established among the various parts. In scholarly
writing, it is a good idea to make the organization of the paper
evident, to describe the structure of the paper. That is,

(1) tell the reader what your thesis is (in a thesis statement),
(2) tell the reader how you will provide convincing evidence to
    support your thesis, and
(3) tell the reader what you did in your research—the problems you
    faced, how you solved them, and so on.

Writing papers is much like teaching. The formula for teaching
is as follows: Tell them what you're going to tell them, tell them,
and tell them what you've told them.

It is helpful to provide charts and tables (infographics) to
show relationships in a clear and obvious manner. Charts and
tables take advantage of our ability to process visual material
in a fast and efficient manner. Let me offer an example. In an
essay on *Star Trek*, it was suggested that the Freudian concepts
of the id, the ego, and the superego can be applied, respectively,
to McCoy, Spock, and Kirk. The id is generally identified with

impulses and desires, the ego with rationality and reality testing, and the superego with conscience.

In the above paragraph, all of the distinctions are buried in the linearity of the written language. The same material can be presented in a chart in which all the relationships are immediately evident:

Psychological Profile of *Star Trek* Characters

id	*ego*	*superego*
impulse	reason	conscience
McCoy	Spock	Kirk

Charts and graphs should be complemented by writing that discusses and expands upon what they show.

Let me suggest a method for making an outline, so your papers will be logically organized and coherent. There are outlining programs for computers, but one can also make good outlines using paper and ink.

(1) Take a sheet of blank paper and cut it into sixteenths. You can do this easily by folding it over and cutting it into halves, cutting the halves into quarters, and so on. You should do this with two sheets of paper, which means you will end up with 32 pieces of paper.

(2) On each piece of paper write *one concept* that you will discuss in the paper. For example, on one piece of paper you might write your thesis. One another piece you will write one bit of evidence that supports your thesis. On another piece you can write another bit of evidence. You should continue brainstorming—writing ideas, concepts, examples, what you will—one to a piece of paper, for as long as you can. If you need more pieces of paper, cut them up.

(3) Organize the pieces of paper in a coherent and logical manner. Some writers pin them on bulletin boards, others stack them and staple them together. The main thing is that by limiting yourself to one idea, fact, concept, or example per piece of paper, you can change the order of matters to be discussed in your paper very easily.

(4) You should have some kind of an introduction section to your paper—in which you give some kind of background and sense of context and do what you can to interest your readers and

stimulate their sense of curiosity. You should also state your thesis—what it is you hope to prove.

(5) The body of your paper should offer evidence to support your thesis.

(6) The conclusion of your paper explains what you have done and offers your interpretation of what you have found—plus any qualifications you have to offer based on difficulties in carrying out your research and related considerations.

Remember that the way you write—your voice, your style— plays an important role in your paper. It is always a good idea to write a first draft of a paper, set the draft aside for a few days, and then revise and rewrite it when you can come to it with a fresh mind. Good writing *always* involves revising and rewriting. First drafts can always be improved, and they often contain a number of stylistic and grammatical mistakes. You should write with a sense of obligation to your readers—you must make your writing as interesting and easy to read as possible.

If the reader is lost, it is generally because the writer has not been careful enough to keep him on the path.

This carelessness can take any number of forms. Perhaps a sentence is so excessively cluttered that the reader, hacking his way through the verbiage, simply doesn't know what it means. Perhaps a sentence has been so shoddily constructed that the reader could read it in any of several ways. Perhaps the writer has switched pronouns in mid-sentence, or has switched tenses, so the reader loses track of who is talking or when the action took place. Perhaps Sentence B is not a logical sequence to Sentence A—the writer, in whose head the connection is clear, has not bothered to provide the missing link. Perhaps the writer has used an important word incorrectly by not taking the trouble to look it up. . . .

Faced with these obstacles, the reader is at first a remarkably tenacious bird. He blames himself—he obviously missed something, and he goes back over the mystifying sentence, or over the whole paragraph, piecing it out like an ancient rune, making guesses and moving on. But he won't do this for long. The writer is making him work too hard, and the reader will look for one who is better at his craft.

William Zinsser, On Writing Well (1976, pp. 9, 12)

11

Avoiding Common Writing Errors

A Note on Communication

When you come to write up what you have discovered in your research projects, you should remember that your main goal is to convey information to your readers in as clear a manner as possible. There are rules that we must obey when we write, just as there are rules we have to obey when we drive. You have to learn the highway code (and pass a test showing that you know the rules) to drive, and have to obey the rules if you don't want to be in a crash. We can get from point A to point B only because we all know the rules and follow them (more or less).

In the same manner, you have to learn the rules of grammar and follow them if you want others to be able to understand you. You can think of punctuation, for example, as being similar (in function) to stop signs, stop lights, direction signals, and so on. If you run a red light, for example, you could get a ticket, become involved in an accident, or both. And if you don't put a period at the end of a sentence, or don't use commas to indicate where readers are to pause, they will become confused.

What you will be doing, for the most part, is telling your readers what the results of your research projects are and how you carried them out. This kind of writing, known as expository writing, need not be dull or bland. But you are not using language the way a novelist does, for example, to entertain readers.

In this chapter we will deal with some of the more common writing mistakes people make. There are certain errors that people tend to make. If you can learn to avoid some of these

113

errors your writing will be considerably improved. It is, of course, impossible to teach you grammar in this short chapter; you should have a good grammar book to use as a reference source, should you have any problems that this chapter doesn't cover. In this discussion, the terms commonly used in grammar will be avoided to the extent this is possible.

Incomplete Sentences (Sentence Fragments)

A number of years ago a Swiss linguist, Ferdinand de Saussure, suggested that meaning is based on differences. The most important aspect of concepts, he said, is in being what others (concepts) are not. What this tells us is that meaning is tied to relationships. Some kind of a relationship between elements in a sentence has to be created for us to find meaning.

If you complete relationships in a sentence (generally involving a subject, an object, and a verb) you can avoid incomplete sentences. The secret is to have two elements (at least)—two people, places, things—and a verb to explain the relationship. Let's consider John, Mary, Rover, and philosophy.

> MARY, who has just returned from a trip around the world, during which she explored the Nile, participated in an archaeological dig in India, and climbed Mount Everest, IS MAJORING IN the subject she finds more interesting than any other (though it won't get her a job)—PHILOSOPHY.

The basic elements in this complicated sentence appear all in capital letters, and they form a complete thought: Mary is majoring in philosophy.

Suppose one were to write:

> Because Mary is majoring in philosophy.

This is an incomplete sentence; the word *because* implies that some kind of description of an act or situation is to follow.

Suppose we were to write:

Because Mary is majoring in philosophy, she will probably find it hard to get a job.

In this sentence, "Because Mary is majoring in philosophy" is tied to "she," which functions as the subject of the sentence and tells us why Mary probably will have trouble finding a job.

Fused Sentences

Fused or run-on sentences are ones that contain several complete sentences that are not adequately separated. Meaning is based on relationships within sentences and among sentences, so it is important that you don't forget to establish this meaning by using transitions and that you don't confuse readers with faulty punctuation. We expect to pause, momentarily, between sentences, and if you tie two sentences together without the right punctuation, the reader can get mixed up.

Here is an example of a fused or run-on sentence:

Mary loves philosophy she might find it hard getting a job.

The problem here is that we have two complete sentences— "Mary loves philosophy" and "She might find it hard getting a job—that are tied together. This problem can be dealt with in several ways. A coordinating conjunction or a phrase could be added to link the two sentences:

Mary loves philosophy, *so* she might find it hard getting a job.

A semicolon could be used to separate the two sentences:

Mary loves philosophy; she might find it hard getting a job.

Note that you cannot use *and* here to join the two sentences because we are dealing, in essence, with cause and effect. *And* would link the two sentences together but would not show how they are related.

Faulty Pronoun Reference

A pronoun is a word used in place of a noun or another pronoun that precedes it. We use pronouns because it would be terribly boring to use a person's name (or any noun) over and over again. There are two important rules to remember when you use pronouns:

(1) A pronoun refers to a noun or pronoun that comes before it (the antecedent). You must make certain that the relationship between the pronoun and its antecedent is unambiguous.
(2) A pronoun must agree with its antecedent in number (singular or plural) and person.

Following are some examples of poor pronoun usage.

Clutching the fried chicken, John got into his car and started eating it.

As this sentence reads now, John is eating his car. We can solve this problem by writing:

John got into his car and started eating some fried chicken.

Here is another mistaken use of pronouns:

Everyone should put their coats away.

In this sentence, the pronoun doesn't agree with its subject. *Everyone* (and a number of other words that seem plural) takes the singular. We should write:

Everyone should put his or her coat away.

Or:

Please put your coats away.

Comma Faults

When two sentences are separated by a comma instead of a stronger punctuation mark (a semicolon, a colon, a dash, or a period, depending upon the situation) or a conjunction, we call it a *comma fault*. A comma signifies a relatively slight pause between elements in a sentence. It cannot separate two sentences, however.

Consider the following sentence:

Mary and John love each other, she got a job so they could get married.

The comma is not adequate in this situation. One of the following alternatives would be acceptable:

Mary and John love each other. She got a job so they could get married.

Mary and John love each other, so she got a job so they could get married.

Because Mary and John love each other and wish to get married, she got a job.

The problem with the first alternative is that no relationships are made evident, so we have two discrete little sentences. We know that Mary and John love each other *and* that Mary got a job. We can figure things out, but it would be better if the relationship were made more evident by a transition or some other device.

Faulty Verb Agreement

Verbs must agree in number with their subjects. This is necessary to make relationships evident. If we have a plural subject and a singular verb, we become confused. Let us return to John,

Mary, and Rover. Let's assume that John loves Rover, Mary loves Rover, and Rover loves both John and Mary.

If we see the word *loves* we know we are dealing with a single subject:

John loves Rover.

Mary loves Rover.

But if we are dealing with John and Mary together (the equivalent of *they*) we must use the plural verb *love*.

John and Mary love Rover.

If we are focusing on Rover (the equivalent of *he*), we use the singular verb form:

Rover loves John and Mary.

The verb *love* is conjugated as follows:

singular	plural
I love	we love
you love	you (plural) love
he/she/it loves	they love

Spelling and Erratic Syllabication

A word is either spelled correctly or spelled incorrectly. The only way to find out whether a word is spelled the way you think it is spelled is to check a dictionary. If you write with a word processor, there is a good chance your program has a spelling checker built into it. You should use this spell checker after you have finished the first draft of your write-up. If you don't have a spell checker or don't use word processing, use a regular dictionary to check any word that you are not certain about.

At the ends of typed lines, words can be broken only in certain places, at syllable endings. The only way to find out a word's correct syllable breaks, for sure, is to use a dictionary. In general, a good rule is to avoid breaking any words into syllables. That way you can be sure you haven't made a mistake in syllabication.

Common Errors Based on Confusions

The material that follows is adapted from my chapter on writing errors in *Scripts: Writing for Radio and Television* (1990):

Two/Too/To. People often become confused when using these words. Here is the correct way to use them:

Too equals degree. "Too many, too few, too soon, too late."
Two is a number. "I want two scripts. I need two actors."
To is a preposition. "I am going to Paris, then to London."

You're/Your. Correct use of these forms is as follows:

Your involves possession. "I like your dress."
You're is a contraction. It ties together *you* and *are.* "That's right, you're correct."

There/Their/They're. These confuse many people also.

There stands for a place. "I'm going there in June."
Their involves possession. "Someone stole their suitcases."
They're is a contraction. It ties together *they* and *are.* "They're a wonderful couple."

Its/It's. Correct use of these is important, too.

Its involves possession. "The fox returned to its lair."
It's is a contraction. It ties together *it* and *is.* "It's my birthday."

Who's/Whose. Correct use of these avoids confusion.

Whose involves possession. "Whose book is this?"
Who's is a contraction. It ties together *who* and *is.* "Who's coming to your party?"

Padding, Wordy Writing

Padded writing uses 25 words to say what can be said in 5 words, or repeats itself and says something two different ways. Students writing term papers often pad because they don't have enough ideas and have to write a certain number of words; they write in a verbose manner and repeat themselves.

padded: I would like to state that I believe . . .
corrected: I think . . .

Incoherent Writing

This refers to writing that doesn't flow, that jumps around and leaves the reader or listener confused. One way to write coherently is to use transitions, which guide the reader along. Transitions tell us what to expect. If, for example, you write "on the one hand" about something, we can expect to find "on the other hand" as well, which will tell us something about the other side of the situation.

Incoherence also is found in primer-style writing. "Look, John. There is Spot. See Spot run. See Spot chase the ball." Primer-style material is constructed of very short, very simple sentences—the kind we find in books written for very young children. This kind of writing is generally inappropriate in works for adults.

Unclear Writing

Unclear writing is hard to understand; it is confusing and ambiguous, at best, and sometimes it is unintelligible. Usually writing is unclear because it contains a number of grammatical errors and because language is not used properly. Sometimes the writing is substandard and does not follow the rules and conventions of English grammar. Such things as run-on sentences, misplaced modifiers, faulty pronoun references, and shifts in person and number can make writing unclear. Sometimes unclear writing has so many things wrong with it that it is hard to know where to start to try to correct it.

Writing should always be clear and intelligible. What happens, in some cases, is that writers forget that they have stored material in their heads that might make a passage clear. They know what they meant to write, but what they put down confuses the reader, who does not have access to this hidden information. In other cases, writers have not learned grammar and cannot write acceptable English.

Awkward Writing

This refers to writing that is stiff and ungainly. Usually this is because the sentence construction and language usage are poor. The awkward writer lacks grace, is clumsy—like a dancer who knows the steps for a dance but doesn't execute them very well.

In some cases, awkwardness is caused by inadvertent repetition of sentence structure ("I believe" followed by "I think" followed by "I want to say," and so on). We find this repetition in cases where a writer has learned only one way to construct a sentence—subject, verb, and object—and this structure is then repeated over and over again.

Reading your papers out loud is a good way to find awkward passages. The best way to deal with unclear or awkward passages is to write new material, rather than try to fix up something that is severely flawed. Rewriting can often save you a good deal of time and effort.

Trite Expressions and Clichés

"Last, but not least," let me end this chapter with a brief discussion of triteness and clichés. You should avoid this material, as they say, "like the plague." Trite expressions and clichés, like the ones I've just used, are shopworn phrases that people sometimes use because they are convenient and understandable. Unfortunately, they are also boring and overused, and you should find other ways of expressing yourself when possible. Sometimes, of course, they express an idea perfectly and can't be avoided, but most of the time you should try to keep away from clichés and trite expressions.

Final Thoughts

In this chapter I have dealt with some of the most common errors people make when they write and problems found with writing. Because of space constraints, I can alert you here only to some of the worst offenders. Every writer should have a good dictionary, a thesaurus, and a grammar book, and should make continued use of them. We all forget, from time to time, the various rules of grammar or how to spell a word. That's natural. But when we write, we have an obligation to our audience to write correctly; that's the least we can do.

If you use a word processor, I suggest that after you have used the spell checker you print out your first draft and make your revisions on the hard copy. Somehow, making revisions at the keyboard, on the screen, just doesn't work very well. And if you revise your papers four or five times, which many writers tell us is necessary, you'll avoid a good deal of eyestrain, too. Remember, also, to double-space all material.

The ability to recognize faulty arguments and to understand why they are faulty is a difficult skill to develop, yet it is an important skill. Faulty arguments are often hard to recognize because they are both appealing and deceptive. They are particularly important objects of study because they attempt to persuade an audience to alter ideas, values, beliefs, attitudes, or actions on the basis of misleading premises or faulty reasoning. Precisely because the purpose of argument is to persuade audiences to accept sound, well-supported claims, we should avoid practices that lead them to base decisions on erroneous inferences and assumptions.

Barbara Warnick and Edward S. Inch, *Critical Thinking and Communication: The Use of Reason in Argument* (1989, p. 127)

12

Avoiding Common Reasoning Errors

Writing and Thinking

The purpose of this chapter is to focus attention on some of the more common errors we make in reasoning—errors that make our conclusions questionable. If people find mistakes in your chain of thinking, they will have good reason to suspect that your conclusions are not correct. Our concerns here are not with formal logic but with "commonsense" aspects of thinking and reasoning errors we make because we are careless or confused.

Writing and thinking are intimately connected. You can be a wonderful literary stylist, but if your thinking is full of holes nobody will take what you write about your research seriously. You may be a great talker, but it is only when you commit your ideas to paper and show people what you have done (and offer evidence so that others can evaluate your ideas) that we can see whether or not your research is of any value and whether or not you make sense. In the same vein, of course, you can conduct wonderful research and be full of marvelous ideas, but if you can't express yourself correctly (using proper grammar), readers of your reports will be skeptical when they are not confused. What follows is a discussion of a number of common errors people inadvertently (usually) make in their thinking.

Stacking the Deck

Stacking the deck involves the use of selected instances. That is, when you make your argument, you use only material that

125

supports your conclusions and pay no attention to material that contradicts your conclusions. (The allusion here is to playing cards. You arrange the deck so the cards are distributed the way you want them to be, and not the way they would be distributed if the deck had not been tampered with.) When you use selected instances, you may be telling the truth but you are not telling the whole truth, and by avoiding certain material you end up with a distorted and incorrect picture of whatever it is that you are describing.

Stacking the deck is not always done on purpose. When Franklin Delano Roosevelt was running against Alf Landon in 1936, a magazine, the *Literary Digest*, took a postcard poll, and on the basis of the poll announced that Landon would defeat Roosevelt. The error the magazine made was in obtaining its list of people to be polled from phone directories, thereby eliminating large numbers of poor people who did not have phones (phones were much more expensive then, relatively speaking, and only the wealthier elements in society could afford them). Roosevelt received 26.7 million votes to Landon's 16.6 million votes in the election. Landon carried only Maine and Vermont, which led to the political wisecrack, often used in discussing presidential elections, "As Maine goes, so goes Vermont."

Inadvertently, then, the *Literary Digest* "stacked the deck" and polled only people who would be most likely to vote for Republicans. You must be careful in making your arguments that you do not (by mistake) end up stacking the deck.

Appealing to Authority

Appealing to authority as proof that certain ideas are correct is generally dangerous. On the other hand, in many cases there is no other way to do things; you can't avoid *some* use of authorities. The world is now so complex that none of us can master all fields and subfields, so we tend, naturally, to look for experts and those who (we hope) speak impartially and on the basis of authority.

There are certain problems involved with the use of author- ity. For instance, is the person an authority in the area being investigated or in a different field? A doctor may be an authority in some area of medicine but may know little about finance or politics. You must use authorities in their fields of expertise or your use of authorities will be spurious.

And what do you do when experts disagree? This is frequently the case. Authorities have different perspectives on some subjects, cite different kinds of evidence, and come to different conclusions. In such situations you can only try to figure out which authority seems to have the best evidence and support for his or her contentions. We often find this kind of a dilemma when we listen to hearings held before some congressional committee. Experts with widely differing points of view testify, and it is difficult to determine who is right. Sometimes, one expert is right about one matter and a different expert is right about another.

The moral of this disquisition is that we must be very careful when we cite authorities. Just because a person is famous or has excellent credentials does not mean that he or she is correct (or doesn't have some ideological or political notions that color his or her view). If you are going to use authorities, as in the case of library research, try to cite the most recent research available from books and journals that are scholarly and not partisan or ideological.

Emotionalism

There is a famous joke about notes a minister scribbled in the margin of his sermon—"Argument weak here . . . shout!" The use of emotionally toned words is a way of trying to avoid logic. If you can get people excited, they won't exercise much discretion and won't be too concerned with whether or not you are telling the truth. We find this technique used a great deal in advertising, where an attempt is made to motivate people to buy certain products or services on nonrational grounds.

Some possible emotional techniques include the following:

(1) *Appealing to people's general prejudices.* Here we use slogans and insulting terms ("better dead than Red"; eggheads) to stir people up.

(2) *Discrediting the person making an argument.* Here we shift attention away from an argument to the person making the argument and attack him or her on personal grounds. This is known as an "ad hominem" (against the man) argument.

(3) *Associating one's point of view with famous individuals.* Here we try to use the prestige of some famous individual (George Washington, Abraham Lincoln, Ronald Reagan, Albert Einstein) to convince people of the correctness of our point of view. An attempt is made to "transfer" belief in the person to belief in an argument—an example of what is sometimes called a "halo effect."

(4) *Bluffing.* Here we use an extremely confident tone to hide a weak argument. Bluffers seem so certain that they are right and argue with such a sense of security that we sometimes get carried along and don't examine their arguments as carefully as we should. Bluffing can be done orally or by adopting a writing style that is supremely self-confident in nature.

Overgeneralizing

The term *generalization* comes from the Latin word *genus* (kind, class) and refers to a statement that is applicable to every member of some class or group. The critical concept here is *every.* When you make a generalization about a group, unless you qualify it in some manner, your statement must cover every member of that group. One contrary instance negates your generalization. Therefore, it is a good rule to avoid using words such as *all* or *every*, unless you are certain that they are correct and that no contrary instances will be found.

Researchers tend to use language that qualifies their generalizations, phrases such as "as a rule" or "tends to be the case" or "generally are." These phrases slightly weaken the generalization and take into account the possibility of contrary instances.

Does this mean we should never use generalizations? Not at all. Generalizations often convey valuable information. A generalization states that certain relationships tend to be constant. We need this information to function in society. If all we do is relate case studies and are too specific, people don't learn anything from what we write. We need to be able to generalize, but we must be careful we don't overgeneralize. That is, we should not generalize from too limited a number of cases studied or examples and we should not make generalizations that are too strong (using "all" or "every").

Statements in Which <u>Some</u> Is True, but <u>All</u> Is Implied

A friend of mine (during my Army days) was a confirmed Anglophile. He wore tweed jackets, smoked expensive English tobacco in his English pipe, read English literature, and dreamed about English girls. By chance he had an opportunity to spend a couple of weeks in England, and he came back a changed man. He thought all the English were like the people he saw on television or heard on the radio—cultivated, aristocratic diplomats and actors who spoke what is called "the received pronunciation" and symbolized England for him. What he found, upon visiting England, was that he held unrealistic stereotypes of the English. There are, of course, a considerable number of English people who speak beautifully, are cultured and cultivated, and who lived up to my friend's expectations. But England (and Great Britain as a whole) is also full of working-class people who speak in a variety of accents (some almost unintelligible to our ears).

My friend had assumed that what was true of some people from England (the diplomats and others he saw on television) was true of all the people in England. On the basis of a very limited and unrealistic sampling of English men and women, he made unrealistic generalizations about what all the English are like. In a like manner, we often fall into the trap of making statements that may be true of some but are most definitely *not* true of all. Often the statements include the word *the*—as in "the English" or "the Jews" or "the Catholics" or "the Blacks"— or *they* (standing for groups of one kind or another). Our minds tend to work by trying to make generalizations on the basis of whatever information we have on hand. All too often, however, we make faulty generalizations and overgeneralize. We call these overgeneralizations *stereotypes* when they deal with groups of people.

What is true of one English, Jewish, Catholic, or Black person is not necessarily true of all—or even most—of them. We must avoid stereotyping people and, in the same vein, making the same kind of thinking error about other matters in which some is true (some Italians are short and dark) but not all is true (some Italians are tall, blonde, and blue eyed).

This "some true/all implied" error is close to the "selected instances" error discussed above, in which generalizations are made on the basis of limited and unrepresentative sampling. The difference is that in the selected instances situation, one chooses selectively from among a variety of examples to use to build an argument; in the some true/all implied case, one just assumes, incorrectly, that what applies to some members of a group applies to all members.

Imperfect Analogy

An analogy is a statement that suggests two things are similar in some important manner. Technically, the term we use for strong analogies is *metaphor* (e.g., the body is a machine); for weak analogies, the term is *simile* (e.g., the body is like a machine). In poetry, metaphors and similes cause no trouble, because we look upon poetry as essentially expressive. In research, metaphors and similes, and analogies in general, are often dangerous because they are improperly applied. (See Chapter 7 for a discussion of metaphors and similes.)

For example, in earlier periods, kings argued that royal rule was natural by suggesting that the state (what we now call a nation or a country) is like a body and needs one heart or brain. Most modern thinkers argue that this is a false analogy; nations do not function like bodies. This analogy is spurious—created to justify the rule of kings. In the same way it can be said that, in certain respects, the human body is like a machine; but this resemblance is forced—it doesn't pay enough attention to all the ways in which the body is not like a machine.

It is perfectly acceptable to make analogies, but it is important to make sure that you do not use analogies incorrectly by comparing things that are too dissimilar or overextend reasonable analogies. When you want to use an analogy, make certain the analogy fits.

Pushing Arguments to Absurd Extremes

This technique involves taking an argument and pushing it to such an extreme that it becomes patently ridiculous. Sometimes we use this technique to attack notions that are contrary to ours; in some cases, we unwittingly push our arguments too far. For example, consider the famous "camel's nose" argument. You must be careful when dealing with camels, the argument goes, not to let them poke their noses into your tent, because once they poke their noses in, the rest of the camel will soon follow. Implicit in this argument is that once a certain thing happens, you cannot limit what else will happen. (This is also known as the "slippery slope" argument.)

You must make certain you don't take some notion you have, which may be valid, and extend it so far (and generalize about it so much) that you lose credibility.

Misrepresenting Ideas

Misrepresenting another person's ideas is caused, usually, by carelessness and inattention. Many researchers make these kinds of slips, which can lead to very serious errors in their conclusions. You must be careful that the material you use accurately reflects a writer's ideas. For example, an author may say something rather general in one paragraph and qualify it in the next. If you do not include the qualification when discussing the work, you may be misrepresenting and distorting the writer's thoughts.

For example, supposing a folklorist writes, "Polish jokes make one basic point—Poles are stupid, dirty, disgusting people. This is quite absurd, obviously." If you were to leave out the second sentence in this quotation, you would be distorting the author's ideas. And if you were to quote only the phrase "Poles are stupid, dirty, disgusting people," you would be distorting his or her ideas even more. Sometimes leaving out just one word (such as *not* or *no*) can lead to major distortions and misrepresentations.

You must be careful to represent any writer you quote correctly. When you use quoted material, it is a good idea to double-check it, to be certain you have quoted the person accurately, and not left out a letter or a line (which sometimes happens). That is why it is a good idea to keep a photocopy of material you will be quoting.

Means Between Extremes

In the United States we believe in compromises—agreements between contending parties in which each gives up something to reach a solution to some impasse. This notion that the mid-point between extremes is correct or acceptable does not work in the area of logic and right reasoning, and can lead to absurd situations. For example, suppose a dictator in a certain country decides to kill all the old maids and bachelors. His wife argues that this is crazy, and he shouldn't kill any of the old maids and bachelors. If he were to decide to compromise and kill only half of the old maids and bachelors, would that mean his position is a reasonable one? Obviously not. Sometimes an extreme position (don't kill any old maids or bachelors) can be correct and a "moderate" position (kill only half of the old maids and bachelors) can be absurd.

We should examine ideas in terms of their merits and of their consequences, not in terms of whether they occupy a position between two so-called extremes or what seem to be extremes.

A Final Note

In recent years a branch of informal logic known as "critical thinking" has become very popular, and there are courses in critical thinking offered at many universities. There are also a wide variety of textbooks on this subject. Those who are interested in this subject and wish to pursue it further are advised to take a course in this subject or purchase one of the many textbooks that are available.

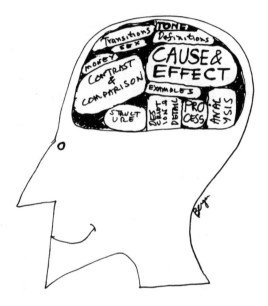

Exposition is writing that explains. In general, it answers the questions how? and why? If we go into any university library, most of the books we find on the shelves are examples of exposition. Philosophies, histories, literary essays, theories of economics, studies of government and law, the findings of sociology, the investigations of science—all these, however different, have for their purpose to explain. Although exposition often is formal and academic, it appears also in magazines and newspapers, in any place where people look for explanations. It is the most common kind of writing, the sort with which we conduct our workaday affairs—the business letter, the doctor's case study, the lawyer's brief, the engineer's report—and the writing with which we attempt to control our world.

Thomas S. Kane and Leonard J. Peters,
Writing Prose: Techniques and Purposes (1986, p. 169)

13

Writing a Research Report

Good Secret Agents
Don't Keep Everything Secret

Throughout this book I have used the metaphor of the researcher as a detective or secret agent, trying to find certain kinds of information. Once you find the information you are looking for, you must tell someone what you've found—otherwise that information cannot be used. To communicate what you have found you will usually need to write a report. There is a fairly standard way of writing up one's research, based on logic and the way our minds work.

Reports give researchers an opportunity to present their findings and to discuss the results of their research. The purpose of the research report is to offer a clear and unambiguous statement of what was done, how it was done, and what was found. The following sections discuss the specifics of how to accomplish this.

The Format of the Research Paper

There is a standard format for research papers; this includes an introduction and sections on methods, findings, and discussion. Each is discussed in turn below.

Introduction. This is a discussion of the problem or subject being studied. Here we offer readers a sense of context, and discuss what was being investigated, whether it was a topic, some question, a hypothesis, or whatever. We also discuss background in this section, including previous research on the subject. The introduction should provide the reader with an overview and situate the research project in a larger context.

Methods. Here we discuss the methods used in the study, describing them in some detail and explaining why we used them. The choice of method is crucial, because each methodology has certain strong points and deficiencies.

Findings: presenting and analyzing data. In this section we present numerical data, or other kinds of data, discovered in our research. In the case of the content analysis of newspaper comic strips, for instance, we offer a table with numerical data to be analyzed. In the case of depth interviews, we might offer representative quotations from interviewees. We must always use appropriate ways of presenting our data or findings, such as tables, figures, charts, or quotations. The important thing is to allow readers to see for themselves what was found. The important thing here is "Show, don't tell."

In this section we also analyze the data and explain their significance. That is, we must interpret what we have found in ways that a reasonable person (our reader) would find plausible.

Conclusions and summary. In this section we draw conclusions, based on our findings, trying to be as honest and truthful as possible. We discuss such matters as problems we faced in doing the research, how our research relates to research on the same or similar topics done by others, what the implications of our research are for the social and political order, and how our research suggests other studies that might be made.

The format of the research paper is designed to shed as much light as possible on how the research was conducted. It is assumed that the researcher is an ethical person who is impartial and is trying to find accurate information. Sometimes researchers have hypotheses (guesses about something) that are tested; in other cases, they want to get more information about some topic or problem. In all cases, however, researchers have a moral obligation to be as honest as possible and to present their findings as accurately as they can. They also must respect the privacy and dignity of any informants used in their research projects.

Style of Research Reports

Reports are written in a formal style, one appropriate to scholarly work. There is some disagreement about whether it is better to write in the third person ("The researcher found") or the first person ("I found"); personally speaking, I see nothing wrong with using the first person. Some people seem to equate a highly formal style with scholarly work, but it is the quality of the thinking and research that is important, not the use of a formal style and jargon. Whatever the case, in formal writing you should avoid a loose, conversational style that is inappropriate.

Research reports should be written in a gender-neutral manner. The best way to avoid having to write "he and she" or "his and her" repeatedly is to use plural pronouns when possible.

Avoid jargon as much as possible. When you use a technical term or an unusual term, define it, so your reader is clear about how you are using it. In some cases, of course, when you are dealing with highly technical matters, it is impossible to write in plain English. You have to judge the fit between your use of jargon or technical terms and your readers.

If you use the first person in your report, you should write in the active voice as much as possible (e.g., "I interviewed three subjects"). If you use the third person it often sounds less stilted to use the passive voice (e.g., "Three subjects were interviewed" instead of "The researcher interviewed three subjects").

Reports are conventionally typed or word processed, using double-spacing with a flush left margin and (for ease of reading) a ragged right margin. Most word processors can easily justify the right-hand margin, but this often leads to wide gaps between words.

Using Quotations and Paraphrases

There is a simple way to avoid accidental plagiarism. If you use words written by others, give those authors credit. You do this by making it clear that you have used their words. We use quotations as a form of "evidence" to show something and also because they state something in a particularly appropriate and distinctive manner.

Quotes of fewer than 40 words. If you are quoting someone and the quote has fewer than 40 words (approximately three lines), the convention is to put quote marks around the material and integrate the quoted material into a sentence. It is a good idea to identify, briefly, the person being quoted. An example follows:

In *Beyond Laughter*, Martin Grotjahn (1966), a Freudian psychoanalyst, says the relationship between comedy and the subconscious is simple since "the tragic guilt of the son is displaced upon the father. In comedy it is the father who is guilty" (p. 86). What he means here is that there is a switch in roles and it is the son who ends up playing the role of the father.

Quotes of more than 40 words. With longer quotes, the convention is to indent five spaces from the place where paragraphs begin, have a flush left margin, and not use quote marks at the beginning or end. An example follows:

In *Beyond Laughter*, Martin Grotjahn (1966), a Freudian psychoanalyst, discusses the relationship that exists between the subconscious and comedy. He writes:

> The thesis is simple, straightforward, and convincing: the tragic guilt of the son is displaced upon the father. In comedy it is the father who is guilty. This inversion of guilt can be seen in Shakespeare's classic comedies as in all others. The villain is the victim of his own villainy. (p. 86)

What Grotjahn means by this is that comedy is connected, in an inverse manner, to the Oedipus Complex, which would explain why comedy is both universal and so important to people.

If you use a long quotation, it should be because you believe the quote has substantial importance for the argument you are developing, and you should point out why you used the quote and why it is significant.

Paraphrasing. We paraphrase when we want to summarize someone else's ideas quickly but don't feel it is necessary to quote him or her. We must be careful not to use the exact language of the person being paraphrased. For example:

> Grotjahn believes that comedy involves an inversion in which guilt is displaced from sons to their fathers. This explains . . . .

The *Publication Manual of the American Psychological Association* (third edition) discusses quotations and citation of quotations in considerable detail. In APA style, footnotes are not used to supply information about quoted material. Instead, the name of the author and the date of the publication (and sometimes page numbers) are included in parentheses in text. APA rules for placement of reference citations are as follows:

- *In midsentence:* End the passage with quotation marks, cite the source in parentheses immediately after the quotation marks, and continue the sentence.
- *At the end of a sentence:* Close the quoted passage with quotation marks, cite the source in parentheses immediately after the quotation marks, and end with the period or other punctuation outside the final parenthesis.
- *At the end of a block quote:* Cite the quoted source in parentheses after the final punctuation mark.

In some styles it is acceptable to put citations elsewhere—for example, before a block quote. The important thing is to be consistent in whatever style you use. If APA style is required for the work, follow the that manual's guidelines.

Reference Lists

The in-text citations are all keyed to a list of references that is included at the end of the report. Such a reference list should include only those sources used in the research project, unlike a bibliography, which also includes works that are useful for background reading.

Every work cited in the report must appear in the reference list, and every work listed in the references must be cited in the report. Each entry in the reference list should contain the following elements (in varying order, depending on the type of work and the reference style followed):

- the author or authors, last name or names first
- the date of publication of the work cited
- the title of the article or book
- for articles, the name of the periodical in which the article was published, as well as volume number and inclusive page numbers
- for books, the city where the book was published
- for books, the name of the publisher

Giving citations correctly can be very complicated. If your instructor wishes you to follow a particular style, you should consult whatever list of guidelines is available for that style and follow it carefully.

Numbers

There are several standard ways to present numbers in text. The rule in APA style is to use words for (that is, write out) numbers less than 10 and use numerals for numbers 10 and higher, though there are exceptions. In tables, for instance, all numbers appear as numerals; and when used in direct comparison with larger numbers, some numbers under 10 should appear as numerals ("3 out of 25 subjects").

Numerals cannot be used to start sentences; often it is best to rewrite a sentence to avoid the problem of writing out large numbers. For example, instead of saying "Thirty-seven out of 42 respondents gave . . . ," you can say "Out of 42 respondents, 37 gave . . . ."

Concluding Your Research Report

You should end your research paper with some kind of a concluding statement. There are two common ways to do this.

The first is to write a brief summary in which you recapitulate your findings and discuss their significance. This is a way of wrapping things up and reminding your reader of what you have done and what you have found. The second is to summarize what you've done and use your findings to arrive at some new insight—a generalization, an idea, a theory—that stems from your research and that may have implications for further research.

The length of your conclusion will be relative to the length and complexity of your research project. For the projects discussed in this book, a conclusion of two or three paragraphs may be sufficient. In longer research projects, which may be quite complex, you will generally need more space to conclude your report.

You may wish to use a "cue" or "signal word"—such as "finally" or "in conclusion"—to indicate that you are concluding your argument. In some cases, it is possible to bring the argument full circle and return to some word or idea mentioned in the beginning of the paper and the problem being discussed. Or you may find some kind of witty remark or clever wordplay that is appropriate. Whatever the case, you must find some manner of ending the paper that will satisfy your reader. A paper should come to a conclusion, not just stop because you've reached the minimum number of words required.

References

Berger, A. A. (1984). *Signs in contemporary culture: An introduction to semiotics.* New York: Annenberg-Longman.

Berger, A. A. (1990). *Scripts: Writing for radio and television.* Newbury Park, CA: Sage.

Berger, P. L., & Berger, B. (1972). *Sociology: A biographical approach.* New York: Basic Books.

Bogart, L. (1985). *Polls and the awareness of public opinion* (2nd ed.). New Brunswick, NJ: Transaction.

Durkheim, E. (1965). *The elementary forms of the religious life* (J. W. Swain, Trans.). New York: Free Press.

Fairchild, H. P. (1967). *Dictionary of sociology and related sciences.* Totowa, NJ: Littlefield, Adams.

Grotjahn, M. (1966). *Beyond laughter.* New York: McGraw-Hill.

Hayakawa, S. I., in collaboration with Berger, A. A., & Chandler, A. (1978). *Language in thought and action* (4th ed.). New York: Harcourt Brace Jovanovich.

Kane, T. S., & Peters, L. J. (1986). *Writing prose: Techniques and purposes* (6th ed.). New York: Oxford University Press.

Kern, M. (1989). *30-second politics: Political advertising in the eighties.* New York: Praeger.

Komidar, J. S. (1952). The uses of the library. In W. J. Goode & P. K. Hatt (Eds.), *Methods in social research.* New York: McGraw-Hill.

Lakoff, G., & Johnson, M. (1980). *Metaphors we live by.* Chicago: University of Chicago Press.

Leon, R. L. (1988). *Psychiatric interviewing: A primer.* New York: Elsevier.

Lowery, S., & DeFleur, M. L. (1983). *Milestones in mass communication research: Media effects.* New York: Longman.

McKeon, R. (1941). *The basic works of Aristotle.* New York: Random House.

Moss, A., & Holder, C. (1988). *Improving student writing: A guidebook for faculty in all disciplines.* Pomona: California State Polytechnic University.

Progoff, I. (1975). *At a journal workshop: The basic text and guide for using the intensive journal.* New York: Dialogue House Library.

Root, R. L., Jr. (1987). *The rhetorics of popular culture: Advertising, advocacy, and entertainment.* New York: Greenwood.

Rubin, R. B., Rubin, A. M., & Piele, L. J. (1990). *Communication research: Strategies and sources* (2nd ed.). Belmont, CA: Wadsworth.

Schwartz, T. (1974). *The responsive chord.* Garden City, NY: Doubleday.

Simon, J. L. (1969). *Basic research methods in social science: The art of empirical investigation.* New York: Random House.

Sjoberg, G., & Nett, R. (1968). *A methodology for social research.* New York: Harper & Row.

Turner, R. (1968). Role: Sociological aspects. In *International encyclopedia of the social sciences* (Vol. 13). New York: Macmillan.

Tosuner-Fikes, L. (1982). A guide to anthropological fieldwork on contemporary American culture. In C. P. Kottak (Ed.), *Researching American culture.* Ann Arbor: University of Michigan Press.

Ward, J., & Hansen, K. A. (1987). *Search strategies in mass communication.* New York: Longman.

Warnick, B., & Inch, E. S. (1989). *Critical thinking and communication: The use of reason in argument.* New York: Macmillan.

Wimmer, R. D., & Dominick, J. R. (1983). *Mass media research: An introduction.* Belmont, CA: Wadsworth

Wright, C. R. (1986). *Mass communication: A sociological perspective* (3rd ed.). New York: Random House.

Zinsser, W. (1976). *On writing well* (3rd ed.). New York: Harper & Row.

Zito, G. V. (1975). *Methodology and meanings: Varieties of sociological inquiry.* New York: Praeger.

Name Index

Subject Index

About the Author

Arthur Asa Berger is Professor of Broadcast Communication Arts at San Francisco State University, where he has taught since 1965. He has written extensively on popular culture, the mass media, and related concerns. Among his books are *Scripts: Writing for Radio and Television* (Sage Publications), *Media Analysis Techniques* (Sage Publications), *Agitpop: Political Culture and Communication Theory* (Transaction Books), *Seeing Is Believing* (Mayfield Publishing), and *Media USA* (Longman, Inc.). *Media Research Techniques* is his eighteenth book and his third for Sage Publications.

Dr. Berger had a Fulbright Fellowship to Italy in 1963 and taught at the University of Milan. He has lectured extensively on media and popular culture—in Denmark, Norway, Sweden, and Finland as a guest of the Nordic Institute of Folklore; in Greece, Lebanon, and Turkey in 1973 and in Brazil in 1987 for the United States Information Agency; and in Germany, France, the People's Republic of China, and England at the request of various universities and other institutions. He is a Consulting and Contributing Editor for the *Journal of Communications*, Film and Television Review Editor for *Society* magazine, Editor of a series of reprints, "Classics in Communications," for Transaction Books, and a Consulting Editor for *Humor* magazine. He has appeared on *20/20* and the *Today* show, and appears frequently on various local television and radio stations in the San Francisco area.

He is married to Phyllis Wolfson Berger, who teaches philosophy at Diablo Valley College, and has a daughter, Miriam Beesley, who is a scriptwriter, and a son, Gabriel Berger, who is working on a Ph.D. in mathematics at Columbia University.

148

NOTES

NOTES

NOTES

NOTES